Trading Spaces
Rooms For Living

Editor: Amy Tincher-Durik
Senior Associate Design Director: Ken Carlson
Project Editor and Writer: Jan Soults Walker
Contributing Art Directors: Chris Conyers, Chad Johnston, Joe Wysong, Conyers Design, Inc.
Contributing Writers: Amber D. Barz, Jody Garlock
Contributing Project Designer: Cathy Kramer, Cathy Kramer Designs
Contributing Photographers: Paul Whicheloe (Anyway Productions Inc.), Jay Wilde
Illustrator: Michael Burns
Copy Chief: Terri Fredrickson
Publishing Operations Manager: Karen Schirm
Editor and Design Production Coordinator: Mary Lee Gavin
Book Production Managers: Pam Kvitne, Marjorie J. Schenkelberg, Rick von Holdt, Mark Weaver
Contributing Copy Editor: Jane Woychick
Contributing Proofreaders: Sue Fetters, Heidi Johnson, Brenda Scott Royce
Indexer: Elizabeth Parson
Editorial Assistant: Kaye Chabot

Meredith₀ Books
Editor in Chief: Linda Raglan Cunningham
Design Director: Matt Strelecki
Managing Editor: Gregory H. Kayko
Executive Editor: Denise L. Caringer

Publisher: James D. Blume
Executive Director, Marketing: Jeffrey Myers
Executive Director, New Business Development: Todd M. Davis
Executive Director, Sales: Ken Zagor
Director, Operations: George A. Susral
Director, Production: Douglas M. Johnston
Business Director: Jim Leonard

Vice President and General Manager: Douglas J. Guendel

Meredith Publishing Group
President, Publishing Group: Stephen M. Lacy
Vice President-Publishing Director: Bob Mate

Meredith Corporation
Chairman and Chief Executive Officer: William T. Kerr

In Memoriam: E. T. Meredith III (1933–2003)

If you would like to purchase any of our home decorating and design, cooking, crafts,
gardening, or home improvement books, check wherever quality books are sold.
Or visit us at: meredithbooks.com

Cover photograph: Paul Whicheloe (Anyway Productions Inc.)

The decorating projects and how-to instructions set forth in this book are not necessarily
endorsed or recommended by the *Trading Spaces* designers and are intended instead
to illustrate some of the basic techniques that can be used in home decorating.

Trading Spaces Book Development Team
Kathy Davidov, Executive Producer, TLC
Roger Marmet, Senior Vice President and General Manager, TLC
Tom Farrell, Executive Producer, Banyan Productions
Sharon M. Bennett, Senior Vice President, Strategic Partnerships & Licensing
Carol LeBlanc, Vice President, Marketing, Strategic Partnerships
Deirdre Scott, Vice President, Licensing
Elizabeth Bakacs, Creative Director, Strategic Partnerships
Erica Jacobs Green, Publishing Manager

Trading Spaces

Rooms For Living

Meredith® Books
Des Moines, Iowa

contents

6 you're in charge!

This introduction offers a glimpse into the exciting makeovers and special features you'll find throughout this book.

Chapter **One**

8 family rooms

Make new memories with a family room that entices everyone to gather around and have fun.

Brush away the cobwebs and turn a museumlike living room into a lovely and livable space.

Chapter **Two**

44 living rooms

you're in charge!

Paige Davis, Host

Joe Farrell, Host

Wouldn't it be great if the *Trading Spaces* crew could come to your house and help you create rooms you would be excited to live in? The *Trading Spaces* designers may not make it to your home; however, this handbook takes you straight to the source, revealing their design strategies with examples that will help you transform ordinary rooms into dramatic spaces you can really live in!

Rooms for Living shines the spotlight on the main living areas to help you make each one functional and stylish. If you desire a space that caters to a more casual lifestyle, turn to "Family Rooms" to find great designs for stylish gathering spots. In "Living Rooms," you'll learn how to create a sophisticated setting to accommodate your entertaining needs. "Bonus Rooms" offers creative ideas for making the most of an attic, a basement, or other extra space. In "Kitchens," you'll see utilitarian spaces transformed by bold color and smart seating solutions. Finally, "Dual-Purpose Bedrooms" shows you how to increase the function of your sleeping area by putting slices of underused space into action for relaxing, working, and more. Each chapter also offers special features:

▶ **One Sofa, Five Ways.** See how an ordinary brown sofa can launch five fabulous looks: romantic, casual, chic, classic, and funky.

▶ **Dos and Don'ts.** Decorating faux pas can happen; this section will keep them from happening to you. Use it to compare design taboos with *Trading Spaces* triumphs.

▶ **Floor Plan Finesse.** These floor plans will help you view rooms with a designer's eye and devise new, smarter ways to arrange furnishings.

▶ **Smart Buys.** Know what to look for before you shop for carpeting, upholstered goods, fabric, wood furniture, and lamps.

▶ **Style Primer.** Discover which style you really love—romantic, casual, chic, classic, or funky—and learn what elements to use to pull the look together in any room of your home.

With all this information at your fingertips, you're as ready for a room makeover as the lucky people featured on the show. Like them, you're about to make your home more comfortable, more functional, and a lot more stylish. And for this special episode, you're the designer in charge!

Frank Bielec, Designer

Barry Wood, Designer

Laura Day, Designer

Amy Wynn Pastor, Carpenter

Laurie Smith, Designer

Genevieve Gorder, Designer

Edward Walker, Designer

Kia Steave-Dickerson, Designer

Christi Proctor, Designer

Carter Oosterhouse, Carpenter

Doug Wilson, Designer

Hildi Santo Tomás, Designer

Chapter
One

family

French
Country,
Hill Country,
Hope You
Love it!
Darrion
Christi

The family room is the space where you gather with the people you care about most, so shouldn't it be a reflection of who you are and how you live? If your family room falls short, check out this chapter to learn how to add personality and functionality to the space.

rooms

Warm glow

Light plays tricks on paint colors, so it's wise to paint a test patch and observe how the color looks at different times of day before painting all the walls. These cinnamon-color walls cast a warm glow in the room; depending on the angle and intensity of the light, the walls can look more golden.

Dressed up

Traditionally, layered window treatments have been heavy, formal-looking ensembles of draperies and sheers. Here matchstick blinds, cream-color side panels, and a fringed valance team up to create a totally different look: casual elegance.

Simple statement

Even though a mantel is merely a ledge, decorating one can be daunting—perhaps because it's a natural focal point, in the spotlight. This mantel is strikingly simple. Featuring a few decorative elements pulled off to the side, it has a clean look and lets the painting be the star.

Smart art

Fabric and artwork are two things that can inspire a decorating scheme. In this case, new fabric inspired a painting. The colors and motifs of the artwork—including the elephant—were gleaned from the fabric used for the valances.

Brown surround

Brown paint transformed this surround, hiding the reddish bricks and helping the fireplace blend into the new scheme.

Fancy that

Home centers and hardware stores are packed with items that can make ordinary furnishings look better. These turned legs stand in for the original ho-hum spindles to prevent the coffee table from looking like a basic box.

Puzzle time

Hobbies are great for doing, but not necessarily good for viewing day in and day out. This clever coffee table solves a puzzling problem: how to keep puzzles-in-progress out of sight. The hinged top folds back to reveal the work surface. The raised sides keep puzzle pieces contained.

DESIGNED BY EDWARD

fit for the family...

Using spicy color and a playful fabric, Edward turns a design-deprived room into a comfy family hangout.

I n the 12 years that these owners have lived in their home, they've put their family room to good use. "We spend all of our family time in there," says one owner. "We play games and do puzzles and watch TV."

They clearly understand what a family room is all about, yet Edward finds their choices a little, well, puzzling. The best features of the room—the fireplace and corner windows—are ignored so Edward assembles a plan to draw attention to these underappreciated assets.

Edward's team coats the walls with cinnamon-spice paint that warms the space and makes the white mantel and surround stand out in style. Reddish bricks on the fireplace surround clash with the traditional mantel and are at odds with the new wall color. A little paint solves the problem. "I am really glad we painted it brown," Edward says. "It works better."

▲ Books are for more than reading—they're great decorating accessories. Stacked or standing solo, they elevate vases, lamps, and more. Here, a single book creates a flat surface for a vase.

▼ A neutral-color slipcover conceals a floral-print sofa and gives it a clean look. Matching pairs of pillows and lamps create symmetry.

◄ Matched sets are nice, but they're not necessary for a pulled-together look. This chair and ottoman wear contrasting slipcovers; the piping on the ottoman ties the two pieces together.

Before
▶ Alabama: Mallard Lake Drive

Problems
▶ Bare fireplace and corner windows
▶ Oddly positioned furniture
▶ Lack of color
▶ Busy furnishings

Solutions
▶ Paint fireplace bricks and dress the windows
▶ Reposition furnishings to balance the room and to emphasize the fireplace and corner windows
▶ Paint walls an orangish hue
▶ Use solid-color slipcovers on the plaid and floral furnishings to quiet the busy look; introduce pattern through fabrics used for pillows and valances

◄ Orange is seldom associated with serenity. Edward's cinnamon-spice wall color borders on orange yet basks in serenity thanks to the bright white mantel and the creamy white curtain panels, which temper the bold color with contrasting coolness.

13

▲ Edward bucks the tradition of boxy bookcases with this circular end table. Books stack around the rectangular base on the lower shelf. The upper shelf holds a lamp that sheds light for reading.

Edward opts for a three-layer window treatment that has a formal yet family-friendly look. This plays up the corner windows. Matchstick blinds introduce earthy texture, creamy white panels define the sides, and a fabric valance sporting elephants and palm trees adds a fanciful touch. In corners near the fireplace, a chair and an inventive end table/bookcase create cozy reading nooks. Repositioning other furniture also helps balance the room, creating better traffic flow and drawing the eye to the main attractions. "The room is now about the fireplace and windows," Edward says with satisfaction.

The remade room reinforces the family's desire to spend time together; everyone finds the space much more welcoming and stylish. They especially love Edward's pièce de résistance: a coffee table with a felt surface for putting together puzzles. Its hinged top keeps puzzle pieces out of sight when the family turns to other activities.

"I can't even believe it's my room," one owner says during the Reveal. "It's such a dramatic change. I have to redo the whole house now."

Window Dressing

Windows come in many shapes and sizes. Here are some tips for dressing windows that stretch beyond the standard rectangular form:

▶ **Corner windows** gain the look of one larger window when dressed with mirror-image treatments. For example, install a swag that swoops to the left on one window and a swag that swoops to the right on the other. If you install draperies or blinds, check that they draw to the outside. In small spaces, avoid fabrics with busy patterns and contrasting colors. Instead match treatments to the wall color so they will blend into the background and create a spacious feel.

▶ **Bay windows** can be dressed in many ways. Like corner windows, they can be visually enhanced with mirror-image treatments. A flexible rod that navigates curves is a nice option for hanging cafe curtains or valances. For a clean look, choose blinds; if desired, add a clean-lined valance. For a formal look, install a rod across the front of the bay and hang draperies on both sides to frame the view.

▶ **Sliding glass doors** present a decorating challenge. The window treatment must allow the doors to open and close freely, yet the dressing needs to enhance the opening and provide privacy and light control. Blinds, fabric shades, draperies, and sliding panels are options to consider. Choose treatments that mount at the ceiling line or that completely draw to the side to keep the doorway clear.

▶ **High windows,** such as clerestory windows, need to be visually lowered and drawn into the design scheme. To bring them down to earth, hang floor-length panels and/or place a piece of furniture beneath them. (A ceiling-to-floor treatment also helps break up horizontal lines.) To make the windows appear larger, install a row of fixed shutters below the windows and operative shutters on the actual panes.

▲ Two $5 footstools, each outfitted with a cushion, flank the armoire, serving as end tables that hold towering earthy arrangements. The $100 chandelier was another of Edward's bargains—and a stylish replacement for a ceiling fan.

Straight ahead

Horizontal stripes make a trendy statement. For maximum mileage let them travel all around a room. These four pictures mimic the wide bands on the plaid draperies and carry the eye around the room. The pictures hang high above the love seat, aligned with one of the upper bands on the fabric.

Great draperies

These wall-spanning draperies can be pulled open to let in light. Mounted to the ceiling on a barely visible white rod, the draperies have a clean-cut, unassuming look. Still, they are dramatic enough to stand up to the fireplace facade.

Sheen scene

Glossy paints are only one way to make a wall shine. An opalescent glaze gives this wall subtle sheen. Rubbed onto the wall horizontally, rather than brushed vertically, the glaze also creates interesting texture.

Feet first

Go ahead—put your feet on the table. Flanked by nightstands, this ottoman forms a creative coffee table, bringing the plaid fabric to center stage.

DESIGNED BY **HILDI**

modern blend

Twice as nice

It's an entertainment center; it's a fireplace; it's ... both! Built around a brick fireplace, this wooden facade with a pine facing gives the room a focal point and maximizes space with cutouts for the TV and electronic equipment.

Monkey business

Every room benefits from a fanciful touch or two—or three. These monkey candleholders are a playful addition yet stop short of silly.

Savvy storage

This nightstand acts as a bookend for the plaid ottoman. Its drawers offer handy storage for CDs and DVDs.

Old homes and modern conveniences are sometimes at odds. Hildi brings function and streamlined style to this living room, while keeping the integrity intact.

Before
▶Tampa: Amelia Avenue

Problems
▶No focal point; too much going on in the room
▶Clutter
▶Awkward furniture placement
▶Harsh white window treatment; dull color scheme

Solutions
▶Create a focal point: a floor-to-ceiling fireplace facade that also houses the television and electronic equipment
▶Edit accessories and create storage to eliminate clutter
▶Reposition furniture to maximize floor space and function
▶Soften and warm up the room with color and draperies

T he owners of this home are caught in a time warp. Though they treasure the architectural detail of their family room, they can't live without their supersize TV or their CD and DVD collections. "We spend a lot of time in this room watching DVDs, watching football, listening to music, and entertaining," one owner says.

Hildi plans to corral all the discs—which are out in the open on metal storage towers—and all the electronics, then she'll streamline the space. Her loftiest project involves building a facade over the brick fireplace—and in the process, covering two original wall sconces the owners love. The project is especially challenging considering neither team has the luxury of a carpenter in this episode (though Paige never explains the absence). Undaunted, Hildi forges ahead with her original design and builds a floor-to-ceiling armoirelike facade that accommodates both the firebox and the electronic equipment. "I love the way the television fits in there perfectly snug," Hildi says, admiring her media center. The streamlined design offers a bonus: Elevating the TV opens up floor space. The CDs and DVDs

▶ While metal towers that hold CDs and DVDs are functional, they're seldom easy on the eye. Hildi creates handsome, handy storage potential in this nightstand. It keeps the owners' music and movie collection out of sight yet close at hand.

▼ Repositioning the furniture and clearing the room of clutter and knickknacks opens up the living space. Placing the sofa at the end of the room helps balance the fireplace facade. Hildi removed the back cushions from the sofa, love seat, and chair and plumped each furnishing with pillows in fabrics featuring the room colors. Because the fabric ate up much of her budget, Hildi didn't have money to purchase an area rug to anchor the space. She borrowed this one from another room.

▲ This grouping of abstract art—actually closeup photos of fruit—picks up the colors in the plaid fabric. The wide white mats echo white trim in the room and stand out crisply against the green walls. Opalescent glaze gives this wall a subtle sheen that mimics the luster in the draperies hung on the other walls. The glaze was rubbed on in a horizontal motion to create visual continuity with the horizontal lines of the fabric.

▲ It's all in the details. Hildi and her team masked off the neutral-color piping on the sofa and other upholstered furniture and painted it burgundy to coordinate with the color scheme of the room. The end table also wears a coat of burgundy.

also find a more suitable home, tucked away in the drawers of two nightstands that serve ably as end tables near the ottoman/coffee table.

Though the fireplace facade gives the room a jolt of the new and now, plaid fabric tempers the modernity. The fabric—$600 of Hildi's budget—wraps most of the walls, creating a soft and lustrous backdrop. "It makes the room so much warmer and cozier," Hildi says. "You just don't want to go anywhere else." The draperies pull to the side, revealing hidden assets, including an arched door with sidelights and a bevy of windows. The fabric also pulls in all the colors used in the room, from the green walls to the burgundy facade to the reddish-orange accessories.

"It's modern, but it's transitional," Hildi says of the new look. Her design satisfies the needs of the owners. With their electronic gear now organized into one stylish space above the fireplace, they are both pleased with the transformation. "It's gorgeous," one of them says. "It's more than I ever thought it could be."

▲ Fabric can launch a new palette or pull together an existing scheme. The olive green in this plaid fabric coordinated with the owners' upholstered furniture and offered several choices for a secondary color. The burgundy won: Hildi used it on the fireplace facade and the end tables. The brighter reddish-orange of the fabric appears as an accent color in some of the accessories.

Must-See TV

Decorating a room around a television can be tricky: Televisions keep getting bigger and making their way into more rooms. Instead of fighting with these big black boxes, factor them into your design:

▶ **Armoires** offer stylish storage for televisions and other electronics. Before building or buying an armoire, measure your TV and other media equipment. Even the newest sleek-looking television may be deeper than you think and may not fit in an armoire. Look for doors that slide into the armoire rather than ones that must be pulled to the sides; slide-in doors allow a full view of the screen and preserve space. Removing standard hinged doors is another option, assuming you're willing to have the TV visible at all times.

▶ **Fireplaces** have become fashionable spots for televisions; some new homes are built with recessed areas above the mantel. Even without a cutout, the wall space above a fireplace is now an acceptable spot for mounting a TV. A flat-screen plasma television, for example, keeps a low profile, taking the traditional place of a painting over the mantel. Some new homes are also packaging built-in media centers next to the firebox, with the mantel spanning both elements. An existing built-in cabinet or shelving beside a fireplace can be retrofitted to create a similar look.

▶ **Pop-up cabinets** are nifty options, especially if a room has lots of windows and little wall space for an armoire. The television sits inside built-in cabinetry and, at the push of a button, rises for viewing.

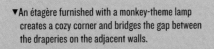

▼An étagère furnished with a monkey-theme lamp creates a cozy corner and bridges the gap between the draperies on the adjacent walls.

23

Rich backdrop

These brown walls wrap the room in warmth. Though not a typical choice for a kitchen/dining area, brown sets the stage for creating a cozy family room from a utilitarian space.

Stitched up

Putting the everyday on display gives a room a homey quality. This antique sewing machine was pulled from its base and placed in a prominent spot on the mantel. The sewing machine cabinet now serves as a base for the dining table.

Shape-shifters

Turnabout is fair play in decorating. These square wall hangings are angled to form diamond shapes that prevent the sitting area from looking too boxy. Old or reproduction ceiling tiles make attractive artwork and can be painted to fit any setting.

Body language

This cozy chair stands silently yet says "relax" quite clearly. Pulled away from the wall and placed at an angle, it visually connects with the dining area and seems to welcome conversation.

Faux fireplace

Old mantels add character to rooms that lack architectural detail. Look for them at antiques stores and salvage yards. Though many sell for hundreds of dollars, this antique mantel was a steal at just $75.

DESIGNED BY CHRISTI

homespun family room

Christi carves a family room out of the dining end of a large kitchen. Rich color and homespun accessories make it a warm and cozy place to gather.

Mission accomplished

Though this Mission-style light fixture seems an odd choice amid country-oriented furnishings, it works because of its earthy colors.

Display space

Some people shy away from buffets because they're big and bulky. This slimmed-down version is actually a sofa table topped with a shelving unit. Though visually lighter than a traditional buffet, it still offers plenty of display space for the family's collectibles.

Gather round

Round tables are great for gathering family and friends, making conversation easy from all vantage points. This 54-inch table is a hardworking part of the room; it can be used for everything from meals and homework to paying bills and playing games. Its base is an antique sewing machine table.

French Country,
Hill Country,
Hope You
Love it!
Darren and Christi

Kitchens that are open to other spaces are the new family rooms. The kitchen featured here opens onto a spacious dining area. "We love the openness and the fact that this room is where the whole family is most of the time," one owner says.

Because the family spends so much time in this kitchen, Christi wants to carve a family room out of the dining area—a space largely eaten up by a big table. Though the area lacks square footage, Christi

plans to put every inch to use to create an inviting family gathering place. "We're going to have a homey room," she says.

Painting the walls brown is the first step to creating a cozy, homey atmosphere. "To me, color is about the feel of the room," Christi says. The brown is a dramatic shift from the formerly yellow walls. However, Christi is confident that the owners will like it, noting that they used the same color in a nearby room. "Doing this,"

► At $75 this antique mantel was such a bargain that Christi didn't even bother to measure to see if it would fit on the wall. It didn't, so Carter removed the mantel top and center divider and sliced the entire piece down the center. After trimming off the ends to ensure a perfect fit, he reassembled the mantel.

▲ It wouldn't be French country without roosters. These plaques formerly hung high on a kitchen wall, but they gain prominence marching down the wall in the new sitting area.

Problems
▶ Cold, barren look that lacks color
▶ Bare windows
▶ Utilitarian furnishings and no elements of comfort

Solutions
▶ Warm up the room with rich color and fabrics; bring in furnishings and accessories that have visual interest and homespun flair
▶ Add window treatments, including a shade that can be rolled down for privacy
▶ Create a comfy gathering spot on the far end of the kitchen

Christi continues, "makes both the spaces appear much larger and more cohesive."

More coziness comes in the form of a cushy chair. Christi positions it near an antique mantel she bought for a bargain. Although the mantel is strictly decorative, it will warm the room by giving the snug sitting area a charming focal point—not bad for an afterthought. "I bought this on a major whim," Christi says. "I didn't even measure it."

Unfortunately, the mantel is too long for the wall. Carter works his carpentry magic to bring the piece down to size without ruining its character. Another clever addition is the new buffet for the dining area: It's actually a slim vintage sofa table topped with a three-tiered shelving unit.

▶ With its glass knob and hinges intact, this cupboard door turned chalkboard has shabby-chic style. Chalkboard paint easily transforms many surfaces into writing spaces. To create a ledge to hold chalk and an eraser, attach a board or a piece of crown molding to the bottom of a cupboard door or other chalkboard frame.

27

▲ "It adds a little bit of Texana to the room," Christi says of this country-style buffet embellished with stars, a nod to the Lone Star State. The oak hutch sits on a vintage sofa table, forming a buffet that's slim enough to fit on a wall near the dining table yet large enough to hold a collection of white pottery.

▶ Table bases usually stand in the shadows; this one is an exceptional standout. An antique sewing machine table supports an MDF tabletop, painted black to coordinate with the iron legs of the antique.

◄ Using different window treatments in the same room can help define different functional areas. This stagecoach shade is a departure from the pendant-style valances on the other windows, yet its understated style and earthy colors are right at home. The shade subtly differentiates the sitting area from the dining area.

▲ One person's fabric scraps are another person's treasures. Christi fashioned this valance by cutting fabric pieces into triangles and stapling them to a board that mounts to the wall. The warm russet and golden tones of the fabric are perfect partners to the brown walls. Amazed by Christi's talent for recycling scrappy fabric pieces, Paige exclaims, "You find a million ways to use them!" "And I'm sure there's a million more!" Christi responds.

Made in the Shade

Fabric shades are a great choice for any window. They're pretty to look at when they're pulled down for privacy, and they soften window frames even when drawn up. Shades can create a variety of looks:

▶ **Stagecoach shades** (sometimes called tie-up shades) are fabric panels rolled or folded up and held in place with fabric ties, ribbon, or cords. The stagecoach shade is unstructured, so it's a good option in casual settings. Because it must be raised or lowered by hand, a stagecoach shade is best used on a window where the shade can be left in the same position most of the time.

▶ **Roman shades** offer a classic, streamlined look. When pulled down, a Roman shade is a flat fabric panel. When raised, the fabric folds into tidy rows. This style is appropriate in any room and can look casual or formal depending on the type of fabric used.

▶ **Festoon shades** look like valances yet function like shades. When raised, a festoon shade forms a curvy valance with abundant folds and two short tails on each side—a look created by the fabric being scrunched up. A festoon shade can be lowered to cover an entire window. It has a somewhat poufed look, so the style works well in romantic spaces.

▶ **Balloon shades** have cascading scallops and big billowy folds. The balloon shade is a showy treatment, so it's best used in small doses. Often these shades are kept in a raised position.

▶ **Roller shades** have made great strides since their white vinyl days. They come in many colors and fabrics, and some have matching valances to conceal the roller. Most often, though, a roller shade is teamed with a separate valance or panels to provide privacy.

◄ Thrift store spindles painted black support the shelves of this hutch, adding old-time charm in the process. The black spindles and stained wood provide an apt foil for showing off the white ironstone pottery.

The weathered mantel and the spindles that support the shelves on the hutch add homespun flair to the room, and an antique sewing machine on display on the mantel consummates the cozy redo. Christi turns the sewing machine table into a base for a new dining tabletop; the black iron table legs inspire the touches of black used throughout the room.

"We have a mix of Grandma's attic, French Country, and new finds," Christi says.

By using many of the owners' accessories, Christi comes in under budget at $974. One owner is pleased to see that her pottery pieces were retained, and she's thrilled with the new mantel. "I always wanted a mantel there!" she exclaims.

TEATIME Artwork focused on Dutch delft conjures images of afternoon tea, an airy patio, and a gathering of good friends and family. The blue and white pottery repeats colors from the sofa.

MATCHLESS GLOW
When everything matches, a room seems formal—and maybe even a little stiff. Choosing lamps with different bases helps the room relax. Matching shades create a subtle visual connection.

CALM COLOR Blue is the color of calm—think of smooth seas and cloudless skies. The floral motif of the deep blue and white fabric used for the slipcover communicates an even more relaxing view. White piping keeps the look smart and not frumpy.

GARDEN-FRESH Real flowers, here and on one side table, partner with a watering can on the other side table to play up the laid-back garden theme.

First Steps to Casual

Do you want easygoing style in your home? Use the elements featured here—garden-inspired accessories, aged paint finishes, and flowers galore—to create a space in which you can kick back and relax.

BASIC BENCH An aged finish on the bench complements the side tables and reassures guests that they can put up their feet and relax.

Before

See the following pages for four additional options:
64, Romantic
96, Funky
I30, Classic
I62, Chic

One Sofa, Five Ways Inspired by the Series

BUTTER UP Pillows covered with sun-kissed golden color lend a cheerful accent to the setting. The sunny yellow hue repeats in the flowers and the popcorn bowl.

FAMILY FIRST Framed photographs of the people you love make a room more personal and welcoming.

AGED PERFECTION Peeling and worn paint finishes always have a tale to tell; their stories add interest to any space.

BLOOMS BELOW
A natural-tone area rug features a smattering of blue flower designs, creating a casual garden underfoot.

Do

DESIGNED BY **LAURIE**

Dos and Don'ts

Mixing Patterns

If the thought of combining three or more fabric patterns in your family room makes you feel defeated before you even start, study these insider tips. They'll help you confidently mix motifs in any room.

34

◀ Laurie perks up a plain sofa in Tampa: Horatio Street using a collection of pillows in three patterns and a solid. As Laurie's fabric choices demonstrate, a good mix of patterns makes a room more interesting and cozy.

Don't

One glance at the pillows in the illustration *above* tells you something is wrong—namely, pattern pandemonium. The pillows feature too many patterns, and none of them have a common visual connection. Here's how to pick a perfect pattern scheme:

▶ **Pattern scale.** Mix three scales of motifs: small, medium, and large. Too many small prints can be dull, while two or more large prints can fight for attention. A family of large, medium, and small patterns will coexist in peace without sibling rivalry.

▶ **Checks and balance.** If you are new to pattern mixing, add a fail-safe geometric design, such as a check or stripe. Wake up a floral sofa, for example, with a couple of striped toss pillows.

▶ **Color connection.** Select patterns within a color palette for pleasing harmony. Patterns don't have to be an exact color match; different shades of the same colors provide visual continuity.

▶ **Style sense.** Maintain a consistent attitude of casualness or formality. Don't mix a formal silk damask with a country gingham, for example. Do mix damask with moiré stripes; pair gingham with ticking.

▶ **Preselected collections.** If you'd really rather not try to create your own one-of-a-kind mix of patterns, investigate pre-mixed fabric collections selected by manufacturers.

Floor Plan Finesse

◀ Barry cleverly uses a long swath of black fabric to create a faux wall for an entertainment armoire in Tallahassee: Emerson Lane. The blue jeans and boots hanging from the ceiling behind the armoire were a planter fashioned by the homeowner. She had even named the planter "Jake." Barry playfully hung the planter from the ceiling so that it looks like Jake is stuck in the ceiling.

Shape a Fabulous Family Room

Plan your family room layout so it's as comfortable for gathering around as it is for watching your favorite films.

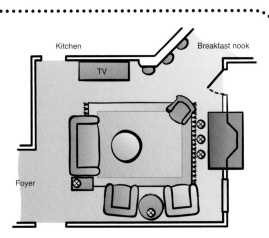

Have Another Seat

Two long walls make this family room convenient for arranging typical family room furnishings. One long wall accommodates a pair of large, comfortable chairs that flank an occasional table. Positioning the sofa perpendicular to the chairs routes traffic from the foyer around the conversation grouping, instead of through it. The wall opposite the chairs holds the entertainment armoire, which houses the TV, allowing more space for seating options—in this case, a third chair. A large area rug connects the various seating pieces. If additional seating is needed for guests, three stools in the breakfast nook can easily join the grouping.

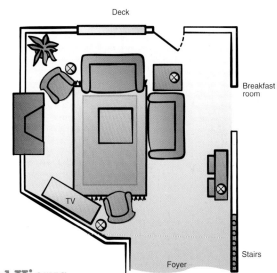

Dual Views

It's always a challenge to position family room furnishings so that the TV and the fireplace can be enjoyed at the same time. In this example, an angled wall offers a solution: Two love seats are placed at right angles opposite the fireplace and the TV (which is located on the angled wall), allowing a dual view. Both love seats are pulled away from the walls. One allows a clear path from the breakfast room to the foyer; the other permits access to a French door leading to the deck. Two chairs—one angled beside the fireplace and another next to the entertainment center—accommodate guests. For still more seating, two benches tuck beneath a console table on the wall between the foyer and the breakfast room. The ottoman/coffee table at the center of the room can also be used as seating.

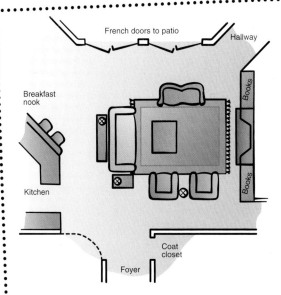

Floor Plan Afloat

What do you do when your family room has few walls and stands in open view of a kitchen and a foyer? A wall of French doors provides a great view and access to the outdoors; however, it can create problems when you're arranging furniture. In situations such as these, consider using a "floating" layout for furnishings. Look for shapely pieces that are attractive from every angle, because all sides will be visible, including the backs. Here, a bench faces off with two chairs, providing visual balance for the pair. The sofa faces the fireplace. Leaving adequate space between the set of chairs and the sofa allows easy entrance to the seating area and makes it inviting. A table behind the sofa softens the view from the kitchen and holds additional lighting.

DESIGNED BY CHRISTI

◄ In Louisville: Roycewood Road, Christi combines upholstery fabrics—a plaid slipcover for the back and a swirling pattern for the pillow and seat—to give this chair a fresh start.

Smart Buys

Upholstered Goods

Whether you buy new or antique upholstered furniture, quality construction and materials are the key concerns, especially in family rooms where pieces will receive a good deal of use.

The old adage about people also applies to furniture: Beauty is often skin-deep. Unless good structure and real value lie underneath, a long-term relationship is unlikely. Before you make a commitment to an upholstery piece, know these guidelines:

The Frame

► **Comfort and style.** As you shop, spend time sitting on each piece you are considering. Do the height and depth of the seat fit the length of your legs? Can you lean back comfortably? Can you easily get in and out of the seat? Are the arms a comfortable height? If you custom-order a piece, ask to sit in one that has the exact same frame and structure.

► **Wood.** Kiln-dried hardwood, such as birch, maple, or ash, is more durable than softwood, such as pine. Particleboard is strong; however, it tends to split and chip.

► **Joints.** On wood frames, look for mortise-and-tenon joints (one piece slides into the other) or dovetail joints (fingerlike projections fit together like gears) that are secured with glue. They're much stronger than butted joints, screwed joints, or glued joints. Check to see if the joints fit together tightly.

Buying Vintage

tip

Furniture at tag sales or thrift stores can be a bargain. If the seller does not know about the construction of a piece, gently lean on the item in different directions to see if it is sturdy. Check for sagging spots and run your hand over the surface, feeling for rough areas. Tip the piece and look for maker and material labels. If the cloth covering the underside is loose, peek at the construction. Also note smells and stains. Dirt is often only surface-deep; if the fabric is unappealing, the piece can always be reupholstered. If smells and stains permeate the entire understructure, the piece will need to be completely rebuilt, especially if it was water damaged.

▸ **Feel.** The piece should not feel light or flimsy. If it does, it may tip easily.

▸ **Sight.** Larger pieces, such as sofas and love seats, should not sag in the middle. Sagging indicates a lack of proper support and bracing. The pieces may eventually sag more or even break at the weak point.

▸ **Coils.** The coils in the seat (and sometimes in the back) of an upholstered piece act much as the box spring in a mattress does. They give the piece firmness and determine how long it will last. Zigzag, wave-shape, or interwoven bands are more likely to sag and lose their shape than regular spring-shape coils. Steel coil springs that are hand-tied where they meet the adjoining coils and frame offer the best stability.

Seats and Cushions

Most large pieces have removable cushions. As you shop, evaluate what will wear best, the look you like, and the degree of firmness you prefer. Decide which of these factors are most important to you.

The highest quality upholstery cushions have an inner core of springs. The springs are generally covered with plain fabric, then wrapped with polyester batting and polyurethane foam; a plain muslin cover protects this ensemble. A decorative cover zips over all components. These cushions are durable and unlikely to lose their shape. However, they tend to be firm and don't encourage snuggling in.

Budget Stretcher

tip

Look for chairs and sofas with hand-tied coils, not crimped springs. For long wear and comfort, choose coils that are tied in as many as eight places. Coils tied in only four places will have a shorter life span, and the springs may pop loose.

Cushions wrapped in down have a soft, cushy, fashionably slouchy look. Though these cushions are comfy, they are impractical for everyday use. Down is not as durable as synthetic materials, and even before it wears out, down flattens.

More common and affordable than down cushions are those made from polyurethane foam covered in polyester batting. A muslin cover is sewn over the cushion; then the decorative cover is zipped in place. As long as high-quality materials are used, these cushions last for years. The density of the foam and the amount of batting determine the firmness of the cushions.

Lower on the quality scale are cushions made from a single piece of polyurethane foam; their decorative covers are sewn on. This type of cushion is less comfortable than cushions with batting. The cushion may shift with the cover, making your furniture appear slightly askew, a look that's hard to remedy. Cushion covers cannot be removed for washing or dry cleaning. However, this construction is generally economical, and the cushions make fine short-term investments for a child's room, a college dorm room, a first apartment, or a guest room. Long wear is unlikely.

At the bottom of the quality chain are cushions filled with shredded foam or pellets. Their covers are permanently sewn in place. If the seams break, expect a snowstorm of messy little cushion innards.

To learn what to look for in upholstery fabrics, turn to page 169.

DESIGNED BY DOUG

Style Primer

(A)

Casual

If you can't wait to get home from a stressful day and put your feet up, casual style is for you. In Tallahassee: Emerson Lane, Doug shapes a room that's beautifully relaxed yet never frumpy. Use these laid-back design ideas anywhere in the house.

Day at the Beach

What could be more relaxing than a day spent on a sandy shore? Doug brings the outdoors inside when he wraps this Florida family room in ocean blue. He makes the room seem even fresher with crisp white trim. The neutral carpeting is the color of sand. (A)

Blossoming Beauty

Spring green blossoms beautify breezy white fabric that dresses the windows. Freehand designs randomly painted on the walls repeat the motif. If you're hesitant to paint freehand, make a stencil: Trace a fabric pattern onto clear acetate and cut out the design with a crafts knife. (C) (E)

Laid-Back Fabrics

Nothing staid or formal belongs in a casual space, including the fabric. For pillows, blue and yellow ticking and a playful paisley print combine with other stripes and solids. (B) (I)

No-Fuss Cover-Up

Finely tailored slipcovers wouldn't visually complement this casual space. Instead, more loosely fitted slipcovers rescue this sofa and chair, but the relaxed look doesn't forgo style. Green piping introduces a designer detail and pulls color from the lotus blossoms to the center of the room. (A) (F)

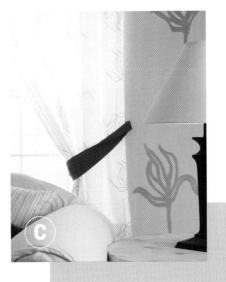

41

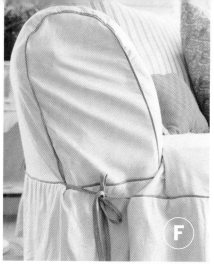

Worn Woods Brand-new furniture has no place in this casual makeover. Painting a white top coat over a dark base coat—and then sanding away some of the top coat— "ages" the console table and coffee table. For a more authentic look, the coffee table top is made of old wood that Faber found. Ⓓ Ⓔ Ⓖ

Sunny Substitutes
The best days at the beach feature plenty of sunshine, so fabrics and lampshades dressed in cheerful yellow serve as sunny indoor elements. Even the abstract painting features playful splashes of yellow. Ⓑ Ⓒ Ⓗ

Outdoor Accents

Outdoor elements emphasize a
casual-style theme. In this room,
an armillary sphere (a teaching tool
used by ancient astronomers) and a
live fern top the console table, bringing
the outdoors inside. The white-painted
finish on the wooden candlestand
repeats the weatherworn look of the
table and other furnishings. (**D**)

Chapter

Two

living

The space labeled the "living room" is often the least-lived-in, least-used room in the house. A living room that is too formal and filled with stiff furniture can be an unwelcoming place with no visitors. If you recognize this design ailment at your house, read on for the cure—elements that will make your living room more stylish and comfortable, such as energizing color, creative architectural upgrades, alluring fabrics, and strategic furniture choices. By following the examples presented in this chapter, you'll guide your living room to an amazing recovery, making it the most-loved room in the house.

rooms

Glorious green

Color speaks volumes in a room, influencing how a space looks and feels. These deep green walls wrap the room like a cocoon and instill richness and luxury.

Blending in

Give something new an aged appearance right now. Olive green stain and gold dry-brushing give this fireplace an old-world look; new tile tones down the former brick surface. To dry-brush, dab a paintbrush in paint, dab off most of the paint onto a paper towel, and then lightly apply the remaining paint to the project, allowing the underlying base coat or natural finish to show through.

This living room says "the more the merrier." Here, Hildi mixes modern, retro, traditional, and old-world styles. It all starts with green fabric.

Retro relaxer

You can take a chair out of the '50s but you can't take the '50s out of a chair. Updated with new fabric and stain, this curvy chair is a welcome throwback to a past era.

Neutral territory

Area rugs often introduce bold color or pattern in a room. In this case, though, a neutral-color rug warms up the wood floor without calling attention to itself, preserving the visual flow among the furnishings.

Golden touch

This linen fabric inspired the green and gold palette. Large-scale patterns work best for window treatments that have gentle folds, such as casually draped panels like these or Roman shades. Smaller patterns get lost in the folds.

Traditional twist

Slipcovers are typically associated with casual style, often because they're loose and unfitted. However, they work on formal pieces too. This snug-fitting slipcover uses dressed-down fabric to relax the formality of the traditionally styled sofa.

Table talk

When pulling together furnishings from different places, look for pieces with similar lines. Like the chairs, this coffee table features clean lines reminiscent of '50s furniture. Sanded and stained, the table looks like the blond wood furniture popular in that era.

DESIGNED BY HILDI

green scene

▼ A strategically placed mirror creates a room with a view. This mirror reflects the artwork on the opposite wall—a grouping of four framed prints above the fireplace. Four identical vases on the chest are filled with green foliage, moving the eye along without cluttering the top. Placed off-center, the vignette gains visual interest.

◀ These gold-color glass vases bring out the golden tones of the chest. The room is essentially a two-color setting, though the greens and golds repeat in different intensities. "I like to keep things simple and I usually don't use a lot of color," Hildi says. Green is designer-friendly because different shades of the color naturally work together.

Before
▶ Louisville: Northridge Drive

Problems
▶ Too much beige
▶ Fireplace too stark
▶ Busy area rug and window treatments

Solutions
▶ Paint walls green and introduce touches of gold
▶ Tone down fireplace by painting it and adding new tile
▶ Substitute a solid-color rug and more-modern window treatments

The owners of this living room describe their decorating style as conservative—and they have the beige walls, beige wing chair, and beige sofa to prove it. "I heard she was the queen of beige," Hildi says of the decorator in the home. "It's not going to be beige anymore."

A contemporary linen fabric with a large-scale leaf motif sets the tone for the room makeover. Hildi matches the wall paint to the deep green background of the fabric. Many people would be afraid to paint their room so dark. However, regarding the color choice, Hildi says, "It's not outrageous." In fact, the dark hue creates a soothing environment.

The metallic gold leaf design on the fabric acts as a majestic foil for the deep green. The fabric is fashioned into casually draped panels that frame the window and preserve light and views

better than the former draperies did. Across the room, the cushions on two chairs feature the same fabric. A snug-fitting solid-color golden sofa slipcover plays up the metallic tones.

The fireplace surround and other moldings in the room also take on a golden glow thanks to a dry-brush technique that enhances olive green stain with a top coat of gold-tone paint. Various wooden furnishings are refreshed and united in a similar fashion. Hildi unearthed the pieces—each with similar forms and

▲ This lamp base complements the leaf motif of the fabric. When selecting a lamp for an end table, consider the visual weight of the base. Choose a lamp whose base makes up about two-thirds of the visual weight of the piece. To prevent the lamp from looking top-heavy, pick a shade whose height (from top to bottom edge) measures less than the distance between the tabletop and the bottom edge of the shade.

Basic Training

Any painter worth his or her stir stick will tell you that having the proper paint and painting tools is key to a successful project. These tips will help you avoid frustration and foul-ups:

▶ **Paints.** Latex paint, a water-base product, has emerged as a favorite for most do-it-yourselfers. It is easy to work with, dries fast, and cleans up with soap and water. Oil-base paints, also called alkyd paints, resist damage from abuse and abrasion and show fewer brush marks. Oil-base paints are often used for doors, moldings, cabinets, and furniture. These paints offer a smooth, rich appearance. However, alkyds also have a downside: They emit odor, dry slowly, require solvent for cleanup, and yellow over time.

▶ **Sheens.** In general, the higher the sheen, the easier it is to clean a painted surface. Sheens work magic in other ways too. A glossy sheen offers reflective qualities that can draw attention to architectural features or brighten a north-facing room. A flat paint camouflages imperfections.

▶ **Brushes.** Natural bristles are usually best for oil-base paints, and synthetic bristles are generally best for water-base paints. Give the bristles a tug to determine if the brush is worthy; if it sheds more than four bristles, find a different brush and conduct the same test. Brushing over a partially dry surface will leave lines, so resist the urge to overbrush. Let the paint dry and then go back over it.

▶ **Rollers.** When choosing a roller, pay attention to its nap. Use short naps on smooth or glossy surfaces and longer naps on rough surfaces. Naps generally range from $3/16$ inch to $1\frac{1}{4}$ inches deep.

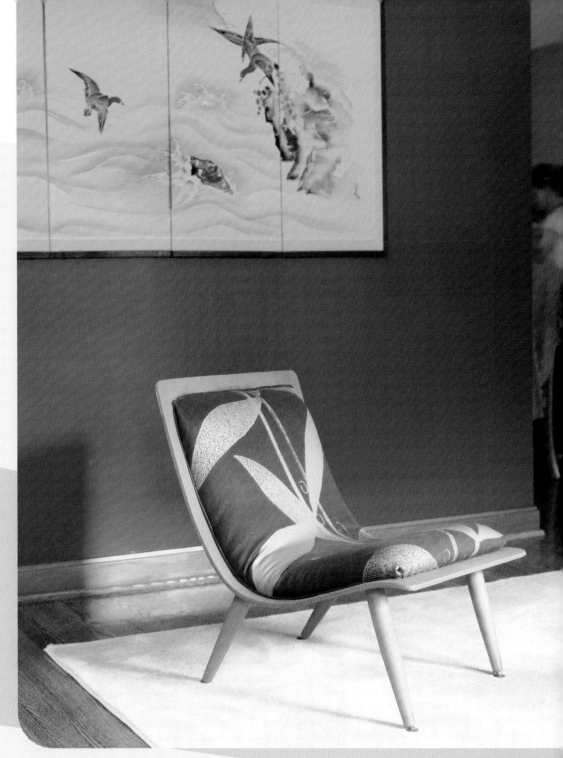

◄ Proper preparation is key to any job. Sanding—and lots of it—helps this coffee table and the other wood furnishings more readily accept stain. Hildi also has her team apply a wood conditioner after sanding so the pieces—though made from different woods—will absorb the same amount of stain for a similar appearance.

▶ Folding screens can be hung on the wall like artwork. This decorative screen gives the room a hint of Asian style.

clean lines—from different thrift stores. "I always try to look at things out of their context," Hildi says. "The expected is what everybody is buying. The artist—the creative person—looks at what it can be."

As room redesigns go, this one is straightforward: The space is dressed with paint, fabric, and carefully chosen furnishings, forgoing elaborate carpentry and the use of themed gimmickry.

The beige blandness is gone for good; the new style is a composite that offers an alluring mix of improvements: more sunlight during the day, '50s flair in the chairs and tables, and old-world touches in the trim and fireplace molding.

The owners are delighted with the inviting new look. "I can live with this," one owner says. "This is beautiful."

Worth repeating

Although mixing patterns is a great way to give a room interest and rhythm, one pattern alone can also do the job. This modern-minded floral fabric repeats throughout the room, helping to streamline a formerly busy space. The soft colors of the fabric prevent the large-scale pattern from becoming overbearing.

Material matters

If you fall in love with an expensive fabric, take a tip from the pros and use it sparingly—as pillows or as a valance, for example. This Finnish fabric inspired the quiet and serene palette. Turned into pillows, the fabric scatters its fresh pattern around the room.

Crowded and cluttered, this living room needs someone to edit and enhance it. Hildi's streamlined design is both sophisticated and family-friendly.

DESIGNED BY **HILDI**

streamlined

52

Birch beauty

A brick fireplace can limit your makeover choices, especially if you're aiming for a contemporary look. This birch facade covers a brick chimneypiece, turning the angled fireplace into a sleek focal point.

Silvery sensation

Gray is a color that labors under many prejudices (think battleship gray or a cold, damp day). Here, gray walls light up near the shiny glint and sparkle of silvery accessories.

Table manners

When sizing up neglected furnishings, look past imperfections and peeling paint and pay attention to size and shape. This coffee table was rescued from someone's garage. It's hefty enough to stand up to the armoire, and its clean lines are ideal for the room. Paint refreshes the piece in an instant.

Making arrangements

Rearranging furniture is a no-cost way to give a room a new look. This armoire was formerly at the far end of the room, partially blocking a doorway. Repositioned in a more central location, it anchors a functional furniture grouping.

sophistication..

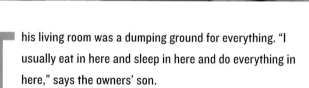

▶ Mirrors can double as artwork. The diamond-shape impressions on these mirror frames introduce subtle pattern.

Before
▶Louisville: Roycewood Road

Problems
▶ Awkward furniture arrangement, including a poorly placed television armoire
▶ Overall clutter
▶ Obtrusive brick fireplace

Solutions
▶ Reposition furniture to create a space more conducive to conversation and watching TV
▶ Streamline the space by removing some of the furnishings and accessories
▶ Build a facade over the fireplace for a cleaner, more modern look

This living room was a dumping ground for everything. "I usually eat in here and sleep in here and do everything in here," says the owners' son.

This multipurpose, maximum use of the space is OK; after all, a living room is for living in. However, the crowded, cluttered look has to go. Hildi's plan calls for creating a family-friendly environment that is streamlined and sophisticated—goals that may seem at odds with one another.

The transformation starts, as so many makeovers do, with fabric—in this case, refreshing fabric from Finland that features a modern floral motif. Soft colors from the fabric begin the streamlining

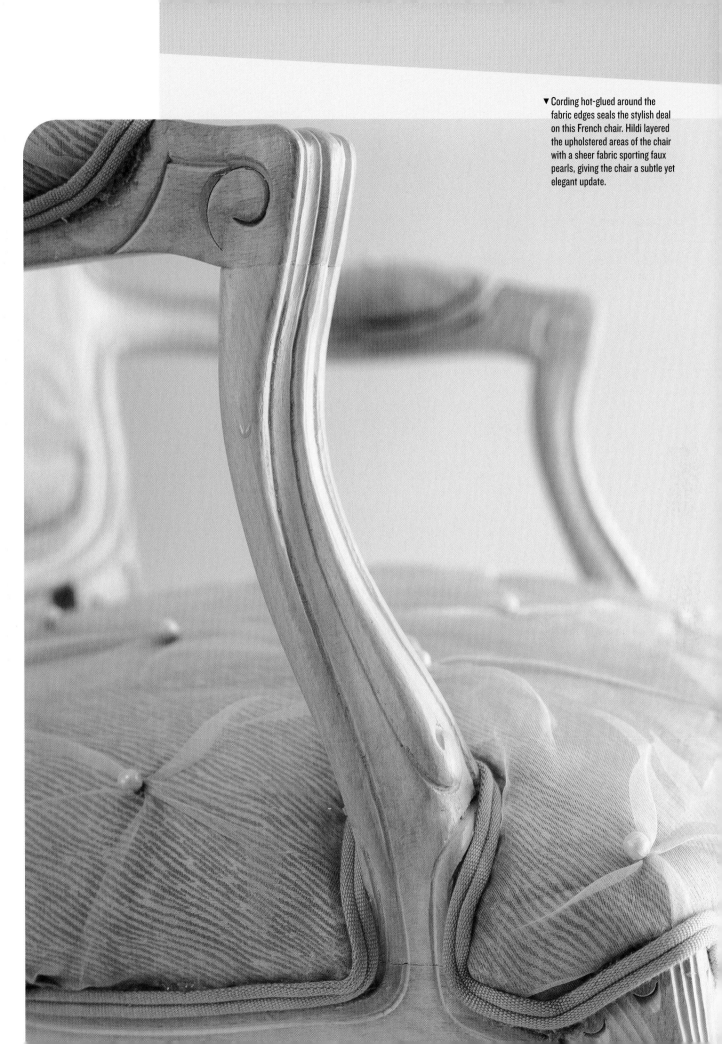

▼ Cording hot-glued around the fabric edges seals the stylish deal on this French chair. Hildi layered the upholstered areas of the chair with a sheer fabric sporting faux pearls, giving the chair a subtle yet elegant update.

Planning Points

Often a space is labeled as a problem room when really the furniture arrangement is causing the trouble. Review these floor plan basics and then consider moving your way to a makeover:

▶ **Find the focal point.** In most rooms, this is the all-important cornerstone of your arrangement. A fireplace, a great view, or a wall of built-ins can fill the starring role. An armoire—especially if it's one that houses a television—or a dramatic painting may also take the lead.

▶ **Establish a flow.** Group furniture to promote a logical traffic flow and to encourage whatever activities you've planned for your room. Halt cross traffic by using seating to create three sides of a conversation zone. Arrange secondary sitting or work areas so they allow easy movement through the room.

▶ **Add or subtract.** Look critically at your existing arrangement. Could you create more floor space by deleting some nonessential furnishings? Would the room be more livable if you added furniture to divide the space into activity centers?

▶ **Break the rules.** Split up a sofa and a coffee table, move a dining table away from the center of the room or pull a bed away from a wall. Unexpected, nontraditional arrangements of furniture can give a room a new look and better function.

▼ If you lack the time to build a crackling fire—or your room lacks a fireplace—set the mood with candles, placed throughout a room or in a firebox. These ivory candles provide a gentle flicker that is reflected in the aluminum-top hearth. Remember, all candles—even small ones and those contained in a firebox—require supervision.

process. Gray paint splashes across the walls, while pale yellow slipcovers update a sofa and love seat. Fashioned into flowing drapery panels and plump pillows, the patterned fabric bridges the gap between the solid colors and gives the room a contemporary Scandinavian vibe. Throughout the room, pale yellow and creamy white punctuate the gray; silvery variations of gray reinforce the scheme. The repetition creates a streamlined effect.

Without a doubt, Hildi's biggest challenge is the fireplace, an awkward angled wall of bricks with a lonely white mantel. Hildi ditches the brick for a birch facade built by Carter. Slate-color stain helps the facade blend with the gray walls, establishing a focal point that quietly commands attention. "The look is much more modern, crisp, straight-lined," Hildi says.

Although the new look is light, fresh, and uncomplicated, Hildi's team encounters some technical difficulties while creating it. The stain on the fireplace facade requires touch-ups to achieve a consistent look. "When you have four people stirring the soup, you're going to get variations," Hildi says.

Despite the difficulties, the makeover is a success. With the armoire relocated to a more central spot and the furnishings edited and repositioned, the space looks and functions better

than ever. Its sophisticated new style is a combination of Scandinavian simplicity, French chic, and breezy vacation getaway. "I can't remember what it looked like before," says one owner, admiring the transformation.

True grit

You don't have to be an expert decorative painter to have stylish walls. New textured paints available at home centers and paint stores make it easy to add depth and dimension to your walls. The sandy texture of these walls was simply rolled on.

Rounding out

Shapely lamps bring a new dimension to the cube-style end tables and coffee table.

A mostly monochromatic scheme (jazzed up with jolts of bright blue) and innovative texture transform this living room. Hildi designs a modern look that fulfills the wishes of both owners.

perfect

Curtain caper

If you want to shift attention from one part of a room to another, create your own drama. Fabric spans this entire wall to form a soft backdrop for the contrasting blue furniture and accessories. The curtain panels rise from floor to ceiling to give the room a sense of grandeur.

Branching out

Folding screens and big potted plants aren't the only way to define wide, open spaces. Wired together, these pieces of bark become swinging art that visually diminishes the width of the double doorway.

Streamlined seat

With cumbersome arms removed, this love seat slips neatly between two end tables. The look is clean and contemporary.

Mod squad

Painted bright blue, this coffee table and matching end tables energize the sitting area. Their clean geometric shapes give the room contemporary flair. Cube-style furnishings may be simple in construction and style, but they make functional display and storage spaces.

DESIGNED BY **HILDI**

harmony

▲ This nine-cubby entertainment center makes
a graphic statement, as well as a nifty corral
for the TV and select accessories. After
depleting 12 cans of spray paint for the
entertainment center, coffee table, and two
end tables, Hildi's team purchased some
emergency latex paint—matched to the blue
fabric in the room—to complete the job.

H e likes his television and the comfort of his well-worn love seat and chair. She likes to surround herself with sentimental things, including her own paintings—and lots of them. Together, the couple's preferences give their living room an undesirable lived-in look. "It's kind of junky, so we want it to have something nice, fresh, new," one owner says. "As long as everything pulls together, I'll be thrilled."

Hildi agrees that the room lacks unity. "It's a hodgepodge," she says. "It has a lot of hers and it has a lot of his, but it doesn't have a lot of theirs."

Hildi plans to harmonize the space with a modern, sophisticated design using texture and a monochromatic scheme. She proposes an easy solution for the fireplace, which has an exposed brick chimney: Remove the tiny mantel and leave the rest as is. "Once we get everything painted, I think this will go away," she says of the obtrusive fireplace.

Indeed, the brick structure seems more at home after the walls are coated with a textured paint that looks and feels like a sandy beach. The beige tone complements the light colorations in the brick; the rough paint texture helps the brick visually recede into the wall.

To draw attention to the other side of the room, Hildi covers a wall—window and all—with faux-alligator fabric. Draped from

▼ Pieces of bark bring unexpected texture to a clear glass vase. Dried grains and grasses fill the center of the vase, creating an everlasting bouquet. To achieve a similar look, place a cylinder or vase in a slightly larger vessel of the same shape and then fill the space between the vases with flat items: bark, buttons, baseball cards, or even photographs.

Before
▶ New Orleans: Carriage Road

Problems
▶ Cluttered look; too many knickknacks and small items
▶ Too much emphasis on the fireplace
▶ Dated and worn upholstered pieces

Solutions
▶ Streamline by editing furnishings and accessories and sticking to one main color and an accent color
▶ Divert attention from the fireplace by creating a new focal point—a fabric-draped wall
▶ Reshape and reupholster the love seat, add a matching sofa, and reposition the furnishings

◀ The walls have a sandy color and a sandy feel. Textured paint adds grittiness that gives the walls dimension. The paint was a strategic splurge: Hildi knew its neutral tone and rough texture would help the brick fireplace blend into the room.

61

▼ The new color scheme is mainly monochromatic; a lone accent color and lots of texture give the room interest. This blue lamp base sports a raised-stripe design that contrasts with the faux-alligator fabric.

ceiling height, the fabric panels bring drama to the wall and create a soft backdrop for a portion of the seating area.

The plaid love seat that had served the couple so well is barely recognizable after Hildi knocks off its arms and reupholsters the shell in a cozy wool fabric. A sofa gets a similar redo. Cube-style tables and an entertainment center—all custom-built by Amy Wynn—provide a stylish perch for the television and well-edited accessories. Pieces of bark are linked to form a textural hanging divider, and a colorful painting done by one of the owners takes a prominent place over the fireplace, ousting a nondescript clock that didn't deserve the prime location. Other paintings are grouped together on another wall, all in sleek matching frames that provide a cohesive look.

The owners return to find an uncluttered atmosphere and a pulled-together look. He still has his comfortable seating, refashioned and freshly dressed. She can enjoy a nicely edited collection of sentimental belongings and paintings. The disjointed "his" or "hers" look is gone; the room is finally "theirs." "Now I guess we better do the rest of the house," one owner says.

Shop for Living Room Storage

If you're shopping for living room storage, such as an entertainment center, check the piece first for stability. If a unit is top-heavy, it is more likely to topple over when filled with books or media equipment. Some shelving units and armoires have adjustable feet to compensate for uneven floors. If yours doesn't, adjust the feet with shims. Some large storage pieces have hidden casters that increase their functionality.

Good-quality movable shelves will be tight and secure yet slide in and out with ease. Check the shelf supports to see if they are strong enough to support the weight of books. Also check the back of the storage unit: Thin wood or cardboard backing is a sign of lesser quality. Choose a unit with a back that is tightly attached, not bowed, for maximum stability.

Drawers with rollers and glides on each side are best; one center bottom roller and glide is satisfactory if the drawer will get only light use. A pull on each side of the drawer front (as opposed to a single center pull) also helps drawers slide evenly. Check that all drawers have a stop so they cannot be accidentally pulled all the way out. Dust liners that form a divider between each drawer are usually found on only the highest-quality furniture. Drawers are often finished only on the front and a few inches on the sides. This is not necessarily a sign of poor quality, although the highest-quality drawers will be completely finished. At all quality levels, unfinished wood should be smooth.

▲ Hildi performed radical surgery on this love seat to create clean-lined contemporary seating. New wool upholstery emphasizes the svelte shape. "It's so soft," Hildi says. "This wool feels like cashmere." Bright blue pillows with a tone-on-tone pattern add a punch of color.

◄ Wire rings connect pieces of bark that form an earthy suspended divider within an open, double-wide doorway. Hildi used a hammer and nail to punch a hole in the top and bottom of each bark piece; then she looped wire through the holes to join the pieces. Stripping bark from a living tree may harm it. Be environmentally friendly and salvage bark from downed or dead trees instead.

SOFT AND CLEAN White paint gives wood pieces a refreshing spin. Scallops and undulating edges keep the look soft and inviting. Wood furnishings with Swedish or cottage styling work well in a romantic setting.

NATURAL INCLINATION
A houseplant makes this romantic composition seem lively and all the more lovely. The four-legged plant stand continues the cottage connection.

First Steps to
Romance

Do you want to add a little romance to your interiors? Use the elements featured here—a soothing color scheme, floral prints, and cottage-style furnishings—to bring that loving feeling into your home.

Before

BLOOMING BEAUTY Floral patterns, on walls, window coverings, or upholstery, conjure up an atmosphere of sunny days and long walks in the garden. The fringe along the bottom of the sofa is a pretty embellishment.

See the following pages for four additional options:
32, Casual
96, Funky
130, Classic
162, Chic

One Sofa, Five Ways
Inspired by the Series

RED HOT Red has always been the color of passion. This ruby red pillow cover draws cozy, heart-to-heart conversation to the sofa. The velvety soft fabric makes the entire sofa irresistible.

SWEET REPEAT Repeating the slipcover fabric on the lampshade prevents the all-white accessories from becoming tiresome.

AIRY ACCENTS Using mostly white accent pieces, such as this dishware, enhances the ethereal feel.

IN TOUCH The rug adds more white to the room. It also introduces pronounced texture that is sink-in soft, creating an inviting romantic mood.

REVEALING LEGS Showing some leg can spark romantic interest. Attractive turned legs make this coffee table easy on the eyes.

DESIGNED BY **FRANK**

Do

Dos
and
Don'ts

Arranging Furniture

Even if a new floor plan is last on your living room
decorating list, read these tips. They may persuade you
to make furniture arrangement a priority.

◄ In Tampa: West Horatio, the homeowners of this living/dining room combination ask Frank to improve the flow of the spaces. Originally, a pair of sofas sat off to the side of the room far away from the fireplace. By pulling the sofas closer to the fireplace and parallel to each other, Frank creates a cozier seating area; he uses the back of one sofa to define the boundary of the dining area without cutting off the flow between the spaces.

Don't

Homeowners often tell *Trading Spaces* designers that they want more comfort in a room. The owners feel uneasy in the space without knowing why. Many of them are surprised to learn that the bulk of their discomfort stems from an inefficient furniture arrangement. When they walk into the new layout, they often exclaim, "We would have never thought of putting the furniture this way!" See if you can spot the arrangement problems in the illustration *above*. Then use the following guidelines to create the best possible furniture

arrangement in your living room. These same design rules can also be applied to your family room or bonus room.

▶ **Position.** Pushing the furniture against the walls creates an unwelcoming chasm between people. (In the room *opposite*, the sofas stand away from the walls, creating an inviting conversation area in front of the fireplace.)

▶ **Traffic paths.** In the "don't" grouping a doorway directs traffic right through the middle of the seating arrangement. Anyone walking

through the room may have to step over legs and interrupt conversation. Again, pulling the furniture away from the walls and into the middle of the room will open up traffic aisles around the perimeter of the room.

▶ **Tables.** In the "don't" illustration the coffee table is far away from the sofa and the chair. Anyone wanting to set down a beverage or a book will have to stand up and take a walk. When the seating pieces are pulled to the center of the room, the table will be more convenient to use. Adding side tables beside seating pieces is another good option.

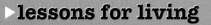

DESIGNED BY **HILDI**

Floor Plan Finesse

▲ When a furniture layout isn't working because the room features too many windows and doors, take a cue from Hildi. In Connecticut: Penny Lane, the living room lacked sufficient wall space to hold the big TV and custom-built entertainment unit. Undeterred, Hildi creates the illusion of a solid stretch of wall by using white-painted bifold doors to conceal one of the windows. The entertainment center now stands in front of the hidden window.

Lay Out a Great Living Room

If your living room is small, make it live large with the help of a great floor plan.

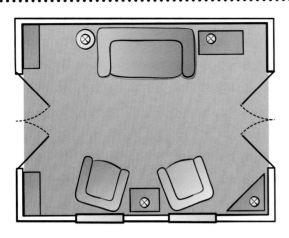

Just Passing Through

Design rules must be broken sometimes. Typically, a room looks and functions best with furnishings pulled away from the walls. However, if you have a small living room with two opposing entrances, your only option is to position furnishings close to the walls and out of the way of traffic. Create a cozy atmosphere by placing a pair of chairs opposite the sofa. Locating the chairs, rather than the sofa, in front of the windows allows slightly more light to filter into the space. In this scenario, built-in bookcases hide behind the French doors on the left; the other furniture is positioned far enough away to allow access to the shelves. To balance the look, a corner cabinet and a tall chest of drawers occupy corners at the opposite end of the room.

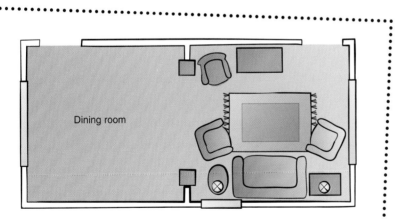

Neighborly Thinking

If you have a small living room connected to a dining room, provide a path for traffic to flow through the space. This floor plan includes a subtle passageway between opposing furniture; a beeline path, though functional, is less stylish. Choosing a love seat instead of a sofa conserves floor space. Angling chairs at each end of the love seat prevents the layout from appearing flat and uninteresting. On the opposite wall, a small secretary stays out of the way yet offers a flip-down horizontal surface as needed. The chair can pull up to the desk or join the conversation grouping. The central area rug visually unites the two halves of the room.

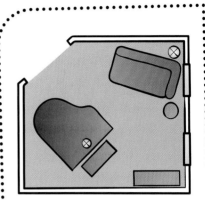

Music Master

Does your builder's master plan have a space labeled "formal living room"? Would you rather use the room for something else? Then forget the label and furnish the space to accommodate an activity you love. In this small living room, a baby grand piano fits into one corner to accommodate a musician. (Pianos are best kept away from exterior walls.) Behind the piano bench a small bookcase holds sheet music and books. In the opposite corner, angled near the window, a chaise offers comfortable lounging for one or cozy seating for two. Two lamps light the space: One sits on the piano for the player; the other stands behind the chaise to serve as mood lighting.

DESIGNED BY GENEVIEVE

◀ In Minnesota: Lakeside Circle, Gen uses the ancient blue bedroom carpeting as a drop cloth, then replaces it with a clever product: large carpet squares. Featuring a geometric design, the squares are positioned so that the pattern is random. Rubber backing eliminates the need for padding, and adhesive dots make installation easy and fast. Tension between the squares keeps them snug.

Quality Ratings

To determine carpet quality, comparison shop among brands by looking at performance ratings. Most carpets are rated on a 5-point scale; a rating of 4 or 5 is best for high-traffic areas. A 2 or 3 rating is acceptable for areas with less traffic, such as a formal living room or guest bedroom. Some carpets are rated on a 10-point scale; 8, 9, and 10 denote the top-rated carpets.

Performance ratings are based on the way the yarns are twisted (a tighter twist enhances durability) and the density of the tufts (the denser the better). Pile height is a personal choice and doesn't affect durability. Heat setting—the process that sets the twist by heat or steam—enables yarns to hold their twist over time and is important only when choosing cut-pile carpeting. (Most nylon, polypropylene, and polyester cut-pile carpets are heat-set.)

Material Choices

The fiber you choose also determines how well your carpet will wear:
▶ **Nylon** is the most popular carpeting material and is available in an array of colors, weaves, and textures. Wear-resistant and resilient, it withstands the weight and movement of furniture and resists soiling and stains. Nylon is a good choice for high-traffic areas throughout your home.

Smart Buys

Carpeting

Carpeting adds warmth and comfort underfoot, and its enticing textures and unifying colors make it an integral design element. When homeowners redo several rooms at the same time, carpeting can become a major decorating expense. Keep these considerations in mind as you shop.

Carpet and Design

tip For a cohesive appearance, select a carpet color that unites existing furniture and draperies and promotes the atmosphere and the look you desire. Pale carpets tend to make a small room feel more spacious; dark carpet colors can help make a rambling room seem cozier. Colors derived from nature, such as sky blue, sea green, earthy terra-cotta, and stone-color neutrals, can complement many decorating styles.

- **Polypropylene,** or olefin, fiber cleans easily, resists static electricity, and is durable. Though it's not available in as many colors as nylon, it is often used in both indoor and outdoor installations because it is resistant to moisture and mildew.
- **Polyester** is a synthetic fiber that resembles wool in texture and has excellent color clarity and retention. Polyester cleans easily and resists water-soluble stains. Oil stains can be difficult to remove. Crushing is possible, so polyester may not be a good choice in rooms with heavy furnishings.
- **Acrylic** feels like wool; however, it looks glossier and is prone to crushing. It is easy to clean and is moisture- and mildew-resistant. It also resists static electricity.
- **Wool** has an obvious texture and resists stains. It can be dyed almost any color, though it is prone to fade in strong sunlight. Wool is somewhat more expensive than synthetic carpeting.
- **Wool/nylon blends** combine the look and comfort of wool with the durability of nylon. They cost less than pure wool. Nylon/olefin and polyester/olefin blends are also available, with varying performance ratings.

The Perfect Pad

Select a carpet pad that suits your new carpet choice. For a cut-pile carpet, choose a pad with a maximum thickness of $\frac{7}{16}$ inch. For a berber carpet, purchase a pad no more than $\frac{3}{8}$ inch thick. Always replace old padding if you want the carpet warranty to remain valid.

How much carpet will you need?

To determine square footage, multiply the length of the room by the width (in feet). Dealers may sell by the square foot or the square yard. To figure square yardage, divide the total square feet by 9. Add 10 percent to allow for room irregularities and pattern match. Given this figure, the salesperson can provide a cost estimate. Ask if the quoted cost includes carpet, pad, and installation.

Have your dealer make final measurements to ensure that you purchase the correct amount of carpet; most retailers offer this service free.

CUT-PILE PLUSH Sometimes called velvet plush, this popular carpeting weave has the loop ends trimmed off. The individual tufts are only minimally visible, so the overall effect is smooth and luxurious. Footprints and vacuum marks will show.

CUT-PILE SAXONY Like plush carpeting, Saxony carpeting has its loop ends trimmed off, but the individual yarns are twisted in a denser, more erect fashion. The well-defined tufts create a little more visible texture and a more casual appearance. Footprints and vacuum marks are minimized.

CUT-PILE FRIEZE In this cut pile, the yarns are extremely twisted, taking on an almost curly appearance. The heavily textured weave gives the carpet a rough, nubby look and minimizes footprints and vacuum marks.

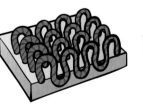

LEVEL-LOOP PILE Woven loops are left uncut, much like the yarns in a loosely woven sweater or scarf. In level-loop piles, each loop is the same height, so the carpet has a uniform look. The loops create a casual, textured appearance that makes footprints and vacuum marks virtually undetectable.

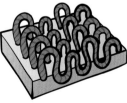

MULTILEVEL-LOOP PILE This weave is similar to level-loop pile: The twisted yarns are left uncut, but the loops are two or three different heights, so the carpet has more textural variety. Most berber-style carpets are either level-loop or multilevel-loop piles.

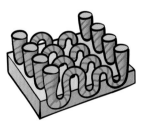

CUT-AND-LOOP PILE This carpet weave combines cut and looped yarns to provide a variety of surface textures, including sculptured effects like diamonds and swirls.

DESIGNED BY **CHRISTI**

Ⓐ

Ⓐ **Style Primer**

Romantic

Romantic style works in almost any room, but the bedroom wears this dreamy look especially well. In Tampa/St. Pete: Bay Laurel Court, Christi uses breezy fabrics and rich colors to make a fairy tale bedroom.

Cozy Palette

Warm colors can make any room more inviting; Christi dresses this bedroom in deep orange, hot pink, and dashes of sunny yellow. Red is another vibrant color that works well in a romantic-style space. At the other end of the spectrum, a palette of pastels can create a more airy appeal. (A)

Sheer Delights

Create an air of mystery and intrigue. In this case, sheer orange panels create a cocoonlike atmosphere around the bed, creating a cozy niche and partially concealing what's beyond. These sheer panels extend from the ceiling and puddle luxuriously on the floor. A similar romantic treatment could dress a window or frame a passageway between rooms. (A) (C)

73

Comfort Plus Christi nestles the bed into a bay window niche, creating a snug getaway. Using an abundance of pillows makes seating or sleeping areas even more inviting. Choose soft and touchable pillow fabrics that exude comfort. (A) (B)

Gorgeous Glow Subtle lighting can make any room more serene and beautiful. One candle sconce on the wall, for example, can lend a fairy tale glow to a bedroom (or any room) when desired. A pendent fixture above the bed and a small lamp on a side table bring understated illumination to this bedroom. At your house, place fixtures on dimmer switches so you'll easily be able to control lighting levels and set a mood that's quiet and relaxing or warm and glowing. (A) (D) (E)

Fresh Flowers Fresh flowers add a vibrant touch. Splurge once in a while on bouquets of your favorite blossoms and use them all around your home. Select flowers in one color to make a simple statement or choose contrasting colors for dramatic impact. (D)

Creature Comforts Include other cozy elements around the house. An overstuffed chair and an ottoman in one corner of the room suggest a quiet evening of reading or a weekend morning of lounging. (C)

Is there undiscovered treasure in your home? If so, this chapter will help you find it—in the form of an underused basement, an attic, a loft, or some other bonus space. If you've left one of these rooms virtually untouched, you're in good company. It can be difficult to know where to begin decorating, so many people simply never start. Here's your inspiration and motivation for making your bonus space both beautiful and hardworking. Do you want to use the area for doing homework, watching TV, listening to music, exercising, or entertaining? Whichever you choose, you'll treasure the results.

bonus

Chapter
Three

rooms

Out on a rung

A trip to a home center or nursery can yield fun finds for decorating a room. Painted and then backed with translucent paper, this garden trellis resembles an Oriental screen and brings style to a humble corkboard.

Bragging rights

Hanging conventional artwork on a sloped wall takes finesse. This large corkboard is lightweight and easy to secure from both ends. Joe hung the Harvard pennant upside down as a joke.

Study hall

With dormers and sloped walls, attics can be tricky to decorate and have the potential for wasted space. This 16-foot-long desk cleverly hits right where the wall begins to angle, its work surface edging out far enough from the wall for adequate headroom. Built-in bookcases are another nifty niche-filling idea.

Knee-high to a kid

A TV tucks into a cabinet in the desk, its low height perfect for kids sitting on the floor or the beanbag chairs.

Clutter buster

Baskets always beat clutter. This wicker basket holds toys, crafts supplies, books, and anything else the kids toss in.

Color connection

Carpeting is expensive, so it may pay to make do with an existing floor covering if it's in good condition. The blue carpeting already present in this room launched the new palette. Teamed with camel and bright blue paint, the flooring is less prominent.

attic retreat

Paint panache

A fun-loving room calls for a playful paint job. Using various paint colors on the different walls is a fresh approach that will appeal to all ages.

Sink in

Beanbag chairs may be a throwback to a previous generation, but kids today still can't get enough of them. Sporting an 8-ball motif, these chairs are as much fun for adults as they are for children.

Defining moment

Area rugs do more than camouflage floor flaws or add color. This area rug defines the kid-friendly hangout spot—one of four distinct areas in the room.

This finished attic is far from done. Seeing a diamond in the rough, Frank gives the underutilized room functionality and style that's fit for a family and fun for kids.

► Bright blue paint accentuates this alcove, where a desk and chair create a nook for quiet contemplation (or harried bill-paying). Frank embellished the drawer front and table legs with a rose motif that has a French provincial feel.

◄ Thermostats have a way of wreaking havoc on a wall from a design standpoint. Seeing beauty where others might not, Frank has his team turn a lowly thermostat into a folk art stick figure. Hook-and-loop tape makes adhering the painted wooden pieces to the wall quick and easy. Spindles, paint stir sticks, decorative rosettes, trim pieces, and more make up the body.

Before
▶ Connecticut: Penny Lane

Problems
▶ Sloped walls; wasted space; limited function
▶ Lack of color, except for the carpeting
▶ Few furnishings and little organization

Solutions
▶ Carve out functional areas in unconventional places, such as in the center of the room, under the eaves, and in an alcove
▶ Splash color on the walls and ceiling, using different colors for different parts of the room
▶ Bring in furnishings that are fun and functional and baskets for storage

The owners of this space are both doctors, and they're desperate to find a cure for their style-deprived attic getaway. "It has no style and it's empty and it has just an inflatable chair, but it has so much potential," one owner says.

Frank sees its potential as a tucked-away family retreat with kid-friendly touches. He devises a plan that maximizes the utility of the room. Rather than doing radical surgery, Frank uses color and furnishings to visually subdivide the room into areas with distinctive functions—some for the kids, some for the parents, and some for both.

In the center of the room, dubbed the "fun area," four beanbag chairs hover around a toy box that doubles as a low-slung table. It's a space for playing games, hanging out, or watching the TV, which is housed in a cabinet built into a desk.

The 16-foot-long desk is the core of the "study area," spanning an entire wall. The TV cabinet in the center visually divides the long expanse; barstool chairs and desk blotters designate

Looking Up

An old builder's adage says it's better to build up than to build on. If you're outgrowing the square footage in your home, think vertical. Finishing an attic in an old house (or the bonus room above the garage in a new home) is often the most economical way to go. Keep this underused area of the home in mind if you want to gain a charming playroom, a soothing master suite, a hardworking home office, or a multipurpose treetop retreat.

▶ **Skylights** naturally brighten a dark attic without disrupting the roofline. Consider energy-saving glass; control light with blinds or pleated shades.

▶ **Furniture** can fit under the eaves, saving space and stowing whatever "cargo" you choose. For a custom look, line walls with cabinetry instead of chests and bookcases. Tuck low-slung seating under the eaves too; then test for adequate headroom.

▶ **Contour** the shape of an attic with thoughtful choices in furnishings and accessories. Visually shorten and square up the typical tunnel-like attic by installing a faux fireplace or a built-in bookcase across one end. Visually widen the space with rugs and diagonal furniture groupings. Create the illusion of height with vertically striped wallcoverings.

▼ The toy box moves out of the alcove and into a place of prominence as a table for the 8-ball beanbag chairs. After adhering painter's tape to the top to mask off random stripes, Frank used a box cutter to cut random wavy lines out of the tape. Frank and the team painted the top camel and then removed the tape while the paint was still wet, revealing the jaunty stripes.

individual study areas for each of the owners' two children. With skylights above each chair, the area also makes a handy art studio or place to do crafts. Decorating from the color in the main area, the wall in the study space is painted a soothing camel color, aptly named "Family Gathering." "When I picked it and looked at the name, I thought 'How cool was that?'" Frank says.

Rich, saturated color defines the "quiet area." Deep blue paint splashes across the walls of an alcove, creating a comforting cocoon. A writing desk and chair tuck into the space, designed for the adults of the house. The owners and their kids may have to take turns using the "reading area," a cozy corner furnished with a sofa, plump pillows, and a floor lamp that stands ready to shed extra light for reading.

At $996.22, this refreshed attic is a bargain. "I think it's phenomenal considering all the stuff I brought in," Frank says. The only problem, notes one owner, is that Frank's design is too big of a bonus to be tucked away from the world. "It's now the best room in the house," says the other.

▲ Slipcovers are ideal for rooms that get a lot of kid action; they can be removed and tossed in the washing machine as needed. This seating piece is larger than a love seat but smaller than a typical sofa, so it required some creative tucking to get the ready-made slipcover to fit properly. Black slipcovered ottomans and a black lamp ground this reading area.

The great divide

Big televisions and exercise equipment can be unwelcome attention-getters. This room divider is a smart solution for keeping those large objects out of sight: A small workout room nestles on this side of the cabinet, while a big television hidden behind doors is housed on the other side.

No sweat

When a furnishing sits in the middle of a room, it needs to look good from all sides. These shelves turn the back of the television cabinet into a hardworking and stylish space for photos and for storing towels to use during an intense workout.

DESIGNED BY **KIA**

divide to conquer

Green peace

Green walls give this room a calm atmosphere (but not so calm that it thwarts good intentions to exercise). The earthy hue was gleaned from the fabric used on the cushions of the sofa and love seat.

Weighing in

Roughed with sandpaper and spray-painted, these dumbbells in the exercise area make a fashion-forward statement.

In the groove

This casually draped swag echoes the curving top of the television cabinet, adding graceful style.

Fabric foray

Compared to fabric-upholstered pieces, leather furnishings have limited color options and minimal pattern. Jazzy fabric replaces the leather on these seat cushions, giving the love seat and sofa the best of both worlds.

This family isn't sure how to tackle their long television room. Kia makes the play, carving out a bonus area and turning the room into two spaces that are equal parts style and function.

Before

▶ Tampa/St. Pete: Sunsplash Lane

Problems
▶ Stark white walls and window treatments
▶ Scattered furnishings
▶ Lack of pattern

Solutions
▶ Cozy up the room by painting walls and adding new window treatments
▶ Divide the long room into two smaller areas with distinct function; group furnishings accordingly
▶ Bring in pattern through a contemporary fabric and a painted rectangular motif

▼ This maze of glaze, as Kia calls it, makes a subtle but strong decorative statement. It matches and balances the visual weight of the large cabinet nearby. The smaller rectangle is done with burgundy glaze, which is rubbed off before it dries to create a subdued color that draws the eye to the framed pictures in the center. To create a similar look, mask off a large rectangle and then a smaller one inside that. Use tinted glazes or a high-sheen version of the paint color on the wall to paint the rectangles. For a high-impact design, paint the rectangles in colors that contrast with the wall.

The owners of this extra upstairs room recognize how lucky they are to have the bonus space, and they want to treat it right. "We're always up here, but it's really boring," their daughter says. "We want to jazz it up."

Kia takes her inspiration from an unlikely source: a treadmill sitting in a corner of the room. The treadmill prompts her to divide the room into two spaces with distinct functions: "One is going to be energizing and one is going to have good nap-ability," she says.

▼ Kia flip-flopped the position of the furnishings, giving the room a new attitude. Positioned by the window in an L shape, this sofa and love seat seem like a big sectional. The mirror echoes the shape of the window and the rectangular motif painted on the opposite wall.

In other words, Kia is going to give them an exercise area and a TV/relaxation area.

A room-dividing TV cabinet is the key component of Kia's design. Faber fashions the massive piece: a wooden box with a sweeping top that brings shapely interest into the long room.

Now for the downside of having an upstairs bonus room: Getting large pieces of furniture up the stairs can be impossible. Such was the case with the cabinet, which Faber has to cut into sections, haul upstairs, and reassemble. "I hope they like it, because I don't know how they're going to get it out of here," Kia says. The cabinet physically separates the two areas and is put to good use on both sides.

On the front, doors pull open to provide prime TV viewing. A rectangular design painted on an adjacent wall balances the scale of the cabinet and adds interest, all for the modest price of paint and glaze.

▲ Mirrors give the exercise area the feel of a real-life gym. The mirrors create a sense of spaciousness and let exercising enthusiasts check their form. Kia originally planned to hang the mirrors flush with one another, but an electrical outlet prevented that. Spaced equal distances apart, the mirrors mimic the look of the rectangular design painted on the wall in the TV area.

Making Arrangements

Teenagers are on to something: Many teens love to rearrange their bedroom furniture on a regular basis, and they aren't afraid to try out new, often unconventional, arrangements. If you're tired of the way a room looks, experiment with new groupings.

▶ **Free up furnishings.** Lining up furniture around the perimeter of a room creates the look of a waiting room. Pull pieces away from walls into close-knit groupings, with major seating no more than 8 feet apart. Create two distinct areas within one room by using an armoire, a tall bookcase, or a folding screen as a dividing wall.

▶ **Group for grandeur.** If furnishings seem too small for a room, group them together for impact. Position a matching sofa and love seat in a tight, slightly overlapping L-shape configuration to create the illusion of one larger piece.

▶ **Consider a fresh angle.** Because a diagonal is the longest line through any room, an angled grouping creates an illusion of width in a narrow room. When positioning a cabinet or another item to create two separate areas, avoid the natural tendency to place it smack-dab in the center of the space. Instead, place it off-center to distinguish the primary space from the secondary area.

◄ Kia sniffed out a bargain with this abstract patchworklike fabric: She paid $12 a yard for the $35 a yard material—a great buy. Besides using it on the cushions and for pillows, she applied it to roller shades to create a coordinated no-sew window treatment.

Behind the cabinet, exercise equipment tucks into a cozy nook with angled walls, allowing the treadmill user some privacy while others watch TV or do another activity. Painted green like the walls, the backside of the cabinet could have been an ordinary flat surface, but Kia dresses it up because it's visible from the entrance of the room: Two shelves are installed to hold accessories and exercise gear. Kia also installs a miniature gym, spending $129 of her budget on weights and other equipment.

With the room makeover totaling $989.90, the gym could have had another dumbbell or two. However, the owners aren't counting pennies—or pounds. "This is awesome," says their daughter who longed for a jazzier space.

▲ Sandy-texture paint gives this wall extra dimension, while tinted glaze adds subtle color and luster. The shaggy floor pillows provide further textural interest.

► The dark stain on the front of this room-dividing cabinet brings richness to the TV area. Bifold doors pull to the side to reveal the television. Taking advantage of all the cabinet space, Kia had small shelves built into the sides; stored objects are partially hidden from view when the doors are open.

Sunny disposition
These yellow walls spread good cheer and have enough oomph to stand up to the black cabinetry and accessories.

Towel time
This metal rack holds towels, which are convenient for workouts and for softening the look of the exercise area.

Abstract thinking
Let common items lying around the house inspire fun and easy artwork. A hockey stick and a skate inspired this trio of paintings.

Table for two
In busy households, many meals are eaten from coffee tables, so the tables might as well rise to the occasion for convenience. This 36-inch-diameter table stands slightly taller than the norm. Two footstools offer seating.

DESIGNED BY **FRANK**

casual compromise

The members of this household have different ideas for their media room. Frank infuses it with personality that pleases the sports-minded males; the woman in the house has her say through pictures that are worth thousands of words.

Stick figures

If you have a passion, bring it into a room. Painted black, these hockey sticks find a perfect home off the ice. Everything from golf clubs and fishing poles to violins and sheet music can double as artwork.

In line

Rectangular black cabinetry takes the focus off the large boxy television and adds symmetry to the space. Hung to match the height of the TV, the cabinetry offers a clean, streamlined look.

Get a grip

Good things come to those who look beyond the obvious. If it weren't for the hockey sticks hanging on the wall, few people would guess that these handles are also hockey sticks—cut down, painted, and hung upside down.

t's a rare room that gives its owners a license to experiment freely with design; usually, nearby rooms demand consideration, and owners need to maintain design flow throughout the house. This upstairs media room has no such concerns. "Since the room is away from the rest of the house, we're ready to go a little bolder," one owner says.

Color is the cheapest route to bold, and Frank has complete confidence in his choice: a yellow that's in the same family as the existing wall color. Frank's more vibrant hue instantly warms up— and wakes up—the room. "It's a very bold, rich color," he says.

With three hockey-loving males in the family, it would have been easy to get carried away with the rest of the room and create a sports pad. However, Frank works in the sports agenda in a creative way that doesn't scream theme. For example, hockey sticks are cut down and painted to form shapely handles on cabinet doors. "I have a thing about objects," Frank says. "Sometimes

▲ If you've got it, flaunt it. Frank turned one owner's photographs into this gallery-style exhibit, aptly titled "Capturing Life."

◄ Upholstered footstools stand in as seating around the coffee table.

Before
▶ Tampa/St. Pete: Sunsplash Lane

Problems
▶ Timid wall color
▶ Disconnected furnishings
▶ Lack of personality

Solutions
▶ Paint walls a bolder yellow
▶ Give the room visual rhythm and a cohesive look with a horizontal cabinet and shelving unit and horizontal-stripe curtains that draw the eye around the space
▶ Bring in items with personal meaning, such as hockey sticks and photos taken by one of the owners

▶ The bold yellow wall intensifies the blue denim upholstery of the sofa. Pillows repeat the colors splashed about the room.

Color Codes

Pink is really only red with some white swirled in. Orange is but a brighter version of peach. When you think of colors as a big family, rather than solitary units, you'll open up possibilities in decorating. Before ruling a color out—or in—consider it in its many forms. Knowing these terms will help:

▶ **Hue** is another word for color. It's usually used to identify a specific color, such as apple green, grass green, or pine green. Black and white are neutrals; they don't have any hue.

▶ **Tint** is a color that has been lightened with white. For example, as you gradually add white to red, you will move from cherry to rose to blush pink—all tints of red.

▶ **Shade** is a color that has been darkened with black. If you add enough black to primary blue, for example, you'll eventually get navy blue.

▶ **Tone,** or tonal value, refers to color intensity—its degree of lightness or darkness.

▶ **Chroma** is the brightness or dullness of a hue. Lemon yellow and butter yellow, for example, can have the same tone (degree of lightness or darkness), but lemon yellow would have a higher (brighter) chroma.

people just go 'Oh, it's a hockey stick.' But if you just spray-paint them and you just relegate it to the shape of the object, it becomes very unique—almost a silhouette."

In that same vein, the modern art that hangs above the sofa is actually the team's interpretation of various sports gear, including a hockey stick and skates. Look closer at the round coffee table, and it takes on the look of a hockey puck. That's by design too.

To give equal time to the woman of the house, Frank devotes one wall to a gallery-style sampling of her photography. The black and white images make a graphic statement and are a perfect complement to the black cabinetry that helps minimize the presence of the large television on another wall.

"I tried to have a space for everybody," Frank says. "I think there's a certain amount of sophistication in the room."

The female owner agrees that the new look is a success. "I love everything about it!" she says.

◀ A stenciled lightning bolt—a team logo—energizes this table, whose round shape mimics a hockey puck. The paint was applied with a pouncing motion, and Frank encouraged the young painter not to worry about perfection. "Sometimes a goof can be more interesting than something perfect," he says. To create an easy custom stencil, lay a paper pattern on top of a piece of poster board or cardboard, cut out the shape with a utility knife, and use the portion with the cutout section as the stencil.

▲ The cabinet doors are a lighter version of the wall color. Frank had his team dilute yellow paint with water (4:1 ratio), apply it to the doors, and rub it off while it was still wet.

◄ Horizontal stripes on the curtains peek out from behind the treadmill and draw the eye around the room. Frank and his team used paint rollers to roll wide stripes onto the draperies, which were spread out on the ground. To create imperfect edges, the team dunked the draperies in water and painted them while the fabric was still wet.

▲ Who would have guessed that a rudimentary stick figure could become a work of art? Fashion similar sculptures by twisting wire from a crafts store into uncomplicated shapes and nailing or screwing the finished piece to a heavy base.

GLOBAL WARMING
Forgo traditional lighting and search for something unexpected. A grouping of paper lanterns, for example, can bring shapely style and punches of fun color into any room.

First Steps to Funky

If you want a space that reflects your wild side, get into the groove with these ideas: bright colors, bold patterns, and hip furnishings. Even your mom's old sofa can be made fun and funky!

UTILITY TABLES The combination of bright colors, playful geometric shapes, and utility chic makes this room fun and functional. This table—constructed of metal and set on wheels for mobility—holds shapely forms that add vertical interest and another burst of color to the room.

COLOR CHAOS Funky rooms let you go wild with color. This fabric sports various shades of pink and orange dots. Pom-pom fringe plays up the dotty motif.

Before

See the following pages for four additional options:
32, Casual
64, Romantic
130, Classic
162, Chic

One Sofa, **Five Ways** Inspired by the Series

IMAGE-CONSCIOUS Art fairs offer opportunities to purchase one-of-a-kind artwork at affordable prices. Look for contemporary artwork with geometric shapes or outrageous abstract designs in colors you love. Build your funky theme around the art.

PLAYFUL PATTERN Retro-style patterns, such as these repeating circles, always work in a funky room. Purchase readily available reproduction patterns or search for vintage fabrics at thrift stores and flea markets.

RETROACTION A trip to the flea market can yield all kinds of goodies for your fun and funky redo. These vinyl-top benches stand in as coffee tables. And check out this "shagadelic" rug!

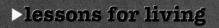

Do

DESIGNED BY LAURIE

Dos
and
Don'ts

Shelf Help

Disown disheveled shelves and use these tips
to create an attractive and orderly display.

◄ In Tampa: Horatio Street, Laurie creates this minimalist display, proving that less is more. The plate and other items become more important when they don't have to compete with a large collection of objects. The subtle backdrop looks like understated tiles (to reflect the homeowners' love of Tuscany); it's actually vinyl flooring.

Don't

You probably have at least one chaotic bookcase at home that is overrun with books and knickknacks, such as the one in the illustration *above*. If so, shape up your shelves with these tried-and-true tips:

▶ **Edit.** Museums pack away objects and art and put out new items on a regular basis. Reduce clutter by rotating your display in a similar fashion. Decide which treasures you most want to see this season, and store the rest for another day. When you tire of a display, pack it away and bring out the next batch of collectibles and books.

▶ **Rethink.** If shelves are adjustable, experiment with shelf spacing so your display can include tall and short items. A large object placed on a center shelf, for example, becomes a focal point.

▶ **Group.** Objects that are similar in kind, shape, or color make a greater impact when grouped together on one shelf. Odd numbers gathered in one spot provide pleasing visual balance.

▶ **Conceal.** If you must stash small, not-so-attractive items on your shelves—such as DVDs and paperback books—hide them in attractive boxes or baskets that will fit on the shelves.

▶ **Layer.** Put tall items at the back of your display and work forward using progressively smaller items. This will give the display depth and dimension. Leave spaces in your display for visual rest stops.

▶ **Elevate.** Use stacks of books, attractive boxes, or small pedestals to vary the heights of other items for more interest.

▶ **Soften.** Reduce the visual impact of banks of books or other straight-line items by including at least one nicely curved item in your display. For example, Laurie included a plate on the shelf *opposite*. Plants and flowers can have the same eye-pleasing effect.

DESIGNED BY **KIA**

▼In North Carolina: Love Valley Drive, Kia adds a wall of shelves to make this family room more functional. Designing the shelves so they step down in height increases interest. Lighting above the upper shelves lends a pleasing glow for evenings. The television is located behind stained-glass-style doors.

Floor Plan Finesse

Bag a Bonus Room

Attics, basements, and rooms above garages can earn a double-bonus rating if they feature a flowing floor plan.

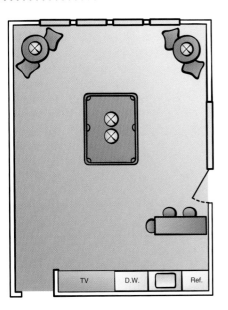

Billiards, Baseball, and Barbecue

A spacious room in a walk-out basement can become the venue for a number of activities. Instead of traditional family room furnishings, consider installing a pool table in the center of the space. (Check with a pool table dealer to find out how much room you need for using the cues.) Use two corners to hold tall tables equipped with stools, where players can wait their turn and enjoy a beverage. In this floor plan, one long end wall accommodates a kitchenette equipped with a small refrigerator and a dishwasher. Add a microwave oven for making snacks in a jiffy. Parallel to the kitchenette, a bar-height countertop and stools separate the cooking/cleanup area from the rest of the room. The large-screen television is located at the end of the kitchenette for easy viewing from nearly anywhere in the room.

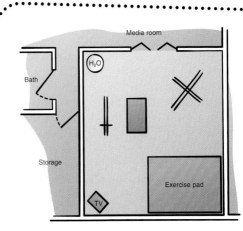

Work Out

If you find it difficult to get to the gym three times a week, consider fitting an exercise room into your basement. This 17×15-foot space features a wide entrance that can be closed off with louvered doors. A large wall of mirrors behind the TV makes the room seem bigger and lets exercisers check their form. Use a swivel shelf and special hardware to suspend the TV from the ceiling so you can see it from anywhere in the room. Face all your equipment toward the TV and mirrors. Tuck a water station into a corner so you can stay well hydrated. A nearby bathroom is a bonus convenience.

Housetop Guest Suite

Guests will feel like royalty when you convert a finished attic into a spacious suite. This scenario defines separate spaces for sleeping, relaxing, and working. Curtains between the bedroom area and sitting room can be closed for privacy or remain open for a roomier appearance. Though the twin beds share a nightstand, each bed has its own bench and dresser. In the sitting room, two love seats—each illuminated by a floor lamp—face a coffee table. Nearby, a chest of drawers offers additional storage and provides a surface for two lamps. A small desk angles into the remaining corner of the room, providing a place for guests to write letters or make telephone calls.

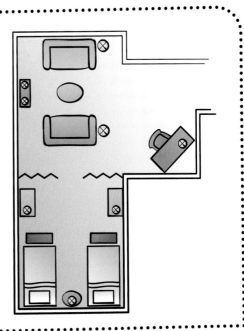

DESIGNED BY **DOUG**

◀ In Tampa: Amelia Avenue, Doug brings style and practicality to this room by including a pair of table lamps with shiny chromelike bases. Flanking the sofa with lamps ensures even illumination for nighttime reading and relaxing.

Smart Buys

Lamp Lighting

Cast your rooms in a whole new light with decorative lamps. When selected and placed correctly, lamps give a room a bright, warm glow and make tasks such as reading, working, and getting ready for the day easier and more comfortable.

Lamp lighting can enhance architectural amenities and disguise problem areas through highlights and shadows. To draw attention to a specific item, such as artwork, place an accent light at a 30-degree angle and focus its beam on the object (the intensity of the beam should be three times the intensity level of general lighting). Spotlighting objects opposite problem areas (such as a corner with exposed pipes) draws attention away from what you don't like and focuses the eye on something more attractive.

For task lighting, choose a fixture with a shade that focuses light in one area. If the shade is open at the top as well as the bottom, it can supplement ambient (overall) lighting. For reading and writing, the diameter of the beam spread out of the bottom of the shade should be at least 16 inches. For more information on task, ambient, and accent lighting, see Light Forms, *opposite.*

Light Output

The type of shade you choose and the light output (lumens) of the bulb determine how much light a lamp gives out. If you experience glare, the light output may be too high. If eyestrain or headaches occur, the light may be too dim. To save energy costs, find bulbs with the light output you need; then choose the one with the lowest wattage.

Shade Secrets

Lampshades spread more light if they have a pale interior. Some retailers code lamps and shades to make it easy to mix and match shades and bases. As a rule, the shade should be two-thirds the height of the base to reveal a small portion of the neck (the fitting between the lamp and the socket) and about one-and-a-half times the width of the lamp base.

Before buying a lamp, ask if you can see it switched on to determine if you like the look and the light output. Place the lamp so that the bottom of the shade is at eye level. When the shade is higher, the glare from the bulb can cause eyestrain; lower lamplight sheds the light onto the surface below it instead of toward the reading or work area.

Keep bases and shades in proportion with the table; if the lamp makes the table appear top-heavy, choose a smaller lamp or a larger table.

Task Light Placement

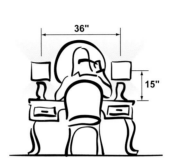

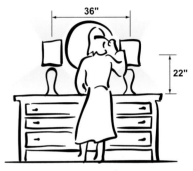

▲ **MAKEUP LIGHTS.** To light a dressing table, add a table lamp fitted with a light-color, translucent shade at each side of the mirror, keeping the light source at about eye level. (Adjust the measurements shown to suit your height.) To maximize the reflective qualities of the lamp, choose a light-color tabletop.

▶ **DESK LAMPS.** For desk work such as bill paying, recipe copying, and letter writing, the bottom of the lampshade should be at about eye level, and the light output from the bottom of the shade should be enough to illuminate all the necessary papers and books.

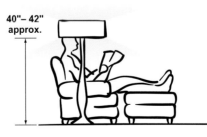

◀ **FLOOR LAMPS.** To read while sitting, position a floor lamp above and over the shoulder for good reading. Short floor lamps, 40 to 42 inches high, should line up with your shoulder when seated. Taller lamps should be set about 15 inches to the side and 20 inches behind the center of the book, magazine, or newspaper you are reading. Check that the lamplight fully illuminates the reading surface without shadows or glare.

▶ **BEDSIDE LAMPS.** To read comfortably in bed, position lamps so that the bottoms of the shades are about 20 inches above the top of the mattress.

DESIGNED BY **HILDI**

Ⓐ

Style Primer

Funky

Even on a gloomy day, a room with funky styling will leave you smiling. Hildi shows you how it's done with eccentric sophistication in Atlanta: Highlands Trace.

104

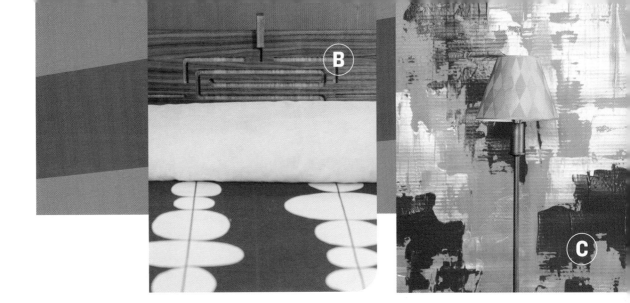

Playful Palette No rule book exists for designing a room with funky spirit, but courageous, bold colors always fit the genre. Here, bright red and a few splashes of yellow turn up the heat and ensure sunny spots throughout the space. (C)

Wall Paper If you really want to have fun with funky, unleash your daring side and experiment with unconventional design ideas. Hildi decides to box up this bedroom with a wallcovering of cardboard sheets—with the corrugated side facing out. One thousand square feet of the brown-paper product cost only $20, making it a bargain surface for any room. (A)

Hip Pattern Fabric festooned in retro-style circles fits the funky theme and adds a fashionable note too. Using the fabric as a comforter and curtain panels adds spice to the room without overdoing it. Use funky-pattern fabric for slipcovers and tablecloths too. (A) (E)

Bed Beauty Funky is all about the unexpected. This custom-built walnut-veneer bed lends a note of Asian-style elegance to the room. Angled into one corner, it becomes an inviting focal point. (B) (E)

It's Art, Baby
A twisting, sculptural lamp base and an abstract work painted directly on the wall issue clear contemporary statements in this oh-so-modern design. (D) (F)

Fashion Furniture
Juxtaposition of unlike elements keeps your mind on alert—another key element of funky styling. In this room, cardboard furnishings in artistic shapes form a hip seating area and offer a dramatic contrast to the chic walnut bed. (A) (D) (H)

Spice and Variety
Touches of red-orange glass—in the form of a vase and a pendent-style lampshade—add touches of '50s glamour. A harlequin-pattern lampshade speaks up with a classic note. Think of funky style as the melting pot of decorating! (A) (C) (G)

Chapter
Four

kitc

Are you dining out more often than usual because you're really busy—or is your kitchen so dreary and inconvenient that you'd rather avoid it? If so, maybe what you're really hungry for is a kitchen that lures you in. If you think you need a bundle of bucks to remake a kitchen, stay tuned to see how the *Trading Spaces* crew does it for less than a grand. You'll learn how to whip up an enticing work core and an eating area that provides space for gatherings of friends and family.

hens

Shelf help

A plain shelf supported with decorative brackets and draped with fabric brings visual interest on high. Everyday dishes or seldom-used items gain display stature when they're artfully arranged in the open.

Leave a message

Black chalkboard paint transforms two underutilized niches into message centers, providing a handy space to jot down the grocery list, notes about school activities, or random missives.

Hello, sunshine

Though the room gets minimal natural light, yellow paint gives the dark kitchen a sun-kissed glow.

Table talk

Black spray paint transforms a $100 metal dinette set. A new, larger top rests on the base to increase elbowroom and match the scale of the space.

DESIGNED BY EDWARD

french connection

Great impostor

Formerly nondescript cabinet doors are cleverly outfitted with translucent ceiling tiles that mimic the look of frosted glass. The inset panels bounce light around the room yet mask dishes and supplies inside the cabinets.

Room with a view

Removing a decorative wooden piece between the upper cabinets that flank the window opens up the sink area and allows room for a Parisian-style cafe awning.

Red redo

Red paint energizes dark cabinetry and helps ground the yellow walls. It also serves as an eye-popping backdrop for inexpensive plates and trivets that dress up the soffit.

Pittsburgh is a world away from Paris, though you'd never guess it from this kitchen. Edward serves up style with a color-happy space inspired by French chefs and sidewalk cafes. The owners? They're saying *merci*.

▲ If life hands you a dingy almond appliance, break out the paint. Edward turned the old fridge into a sleek two-tone tower that's in tune with the times. He gave the doors a silvery finish and sprayed the sides and top black, using specially formulated appliance paints. He also transformed the stove with black paint designed to withstand high temperatures.

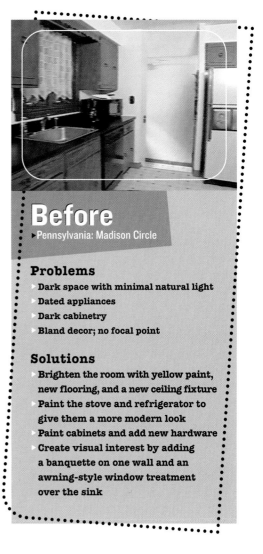

◄ Though often overlooked, flat-panel doors are blank canvases with decorating potential. The chef Edward painted on this door puts a fun exclamation point on his French-inspired design and keeps the room from taking itself too seriously.

Before
▶ Pennsylvania: Madison Circle

Problems
▶ Dark space with minimal natural light
▶ Dated appliances
▶ Dark cabinetry
▶ Bland decor; no focal point

Solutions
▶ Brighten the room with yellow paint, new flooring, and a new ceiling fixture
▶ Paint the stove and refrigerator to give them a more modern look
▶ Paint cabinets and add new hardware
▶ Create visual interest by adding a banquette on one wall and an awning-style window treatment over the sink

With its dated appliances, dark cabinets, and overall drab disposition, this kitchen has been simmering way too long in a bygone era. The owners are eager to turn in their style-deprived space for a mystery makeover. They're ready for anything—except whimsical. "Whimsical seems fake," the husband notes.

Enter Edward, who attaches a name to his vision for the room. "I'm calling it Whimsical Chef," he declares. This could have been a recipe for disaster, but Edward wisely keeps the whimsy in check. The friendly French chef he paints on a pocket door can slide out of sight if the owners want to hide the lighthearted rendering. In his absence, the remade kitchen has the feel of a chic Parisian cafe. A black and white checked awning hangs above the kitchen sink window, providing a focal point on a wall that previously lacked

interest. The same checked fabric covers the seat on the bracketed banquette, which is plumped with pillows to cushion up to eight seated guests. On the walls near the table, chalkboard paint transforms little-used niches into message boards.

Beyond the smaller improvements, the outdated appliances and cabinets still loom large. The flooring, though not as much of a

◄ Little details make a difference. Instead of a traditional bench-style banquette with legs, Edward designed this sleek seating that attaches to the wall with brackets and 2×2s and seems to float in air. A band of red fabric and black piping add dressmaker detailing to the cushion.

misfit, also needs an update. Edward ingeniously addresses all three of these common maladies while staying within his $1,000 budget. The stove and refrigerator find their contemporary footing with black and silver paints designed for appliances. Peel-and-stick

tiles placed over the existing flooring lighten and update the space. Bright red paint energizes the dark cabinetry.

Edward's invigorating palette is the most dramatic change in the room, though the paint job is a fairly easy one. In addition to the red cabinets, Edward transforms bland white walls with warm yellow paint, a nod to French-country style. "They said it was dark in here and didn't get a lot of sun, so I thought, 'Well, we'll just make it yellow and bring in sunshine every day,'" Edward says.

Indeed, the kitchen radiates friendly warmth in many ways. An inexpensive table outfitted with a big new laminate top beckons family and friends to gather round. Trivets and plates with motifs

Bold Strokes

Vibrant color makes any room sizzle. Why, then, do so many walls languish in boring beige and wishy-washy white? Fear of the unknown may be a factor; if it's your factor, arm yourself with know-how: Consider these points before committing to a strong color:

▶ **Determine the mood you want to evoke.** Warm colors, such as red and yellow, create a sense of coziness and comfort. They also energize, so they're good choices for kitchens, family rooms, and other active spaces. Cool colors, such as blue and green, soothe and relax. They're good for rooms where calm is desired, such as bedrooms or home offices.

▶ **Find a color partner.** Although choosing one bold color may seem challenging enough, you'll need to choose a second and even a third equally strong color to keep the room interesting. These additional colors will actually help ground the dominant hue.

▶ **Evaluate light and space.** North-facing rooms or areas without windows benefit from warm colors, such as reds and yellows. These colors help cozy up the space and visually bring a large area down in size. For sunny spaces or small rooms that could use a feeling of airiness, consider cool colors, such as blue and green.

▶ **Let color be your building blocks.** Use bold color to draw attention to an architectural feature, such as a fireplace, chair rail, or window trim. If you'd rather not paint the more permanent parts of a room, reserve the strong color for an end table or chair. Even a small dose of color will command attention.

▶ **Remember that color is a personal choice.** Consider only the colors that please you; forget trends and the preferences of the paint salesperson. For some people, that may be invigorating orange; for others it may be mossy green. Think of colors that evoke happy memories for you—the turquoise blue of an ocean or the brilliant greens of a garden, for example. The clothes hanging in your closet are a good indicator of your personal color preferences.

▼ Invigorating color is great for rooms where the activity level is high. This kitchen wears a bold but classic color combo: yellow and red with touches of black and white. Though pattern and artwork are minimal, the black and white checked fabric makes a big graphic statement. To add depth to the yellow walls, Edward and his team dipped a whisk broom in darker yellow paint that had a hint of orange and lightly dragged it across the surface.

of chefs and grapes adorn the walls, and a shelf holding dishware furthers the casual French feel.

"My mission was to give their three boys who eat breakfast and lunch in here every day a space that they could enjoy," Edward explains. "The rest of the house is Mom and Dad's space."

The grown-ups get a virtually brand-new kitchen, with the microwave oven and coffeepot being about the only things returned to the room. The owners are thrilled with the transformation, whimsy and all. "This is incredible," one of the owners says. "It's beautiful. This is something I could have never done on my own."

Tile style

White paneling instantly refreshes the walls—and for that matter, the entire room. The paneling mimics the look of tile minus its tough-to-clean grout.

Blue skies

The ceiling gets the royal treatment: upbeat blue paint that contrasts with the white walls and cabinetry. The intense color gives the room drama. A new fixture mounted flush with the ceiling replaces a hanging light, keeping the line of sight unobstructed.

Blind ambition

Clean-lined horizontal blinds dress the windows and quietly blend with the walls. Unfettered by fabric treatments, the bay—and the view out the windows—becomes the focus.

Have a seat

An impressive banquette follows the contours of the bay, becoming the focal point of the room. Foam cushions and a smattering of pillows offer sink-in comfort.

Main menu

A custom-made message center created with chalkboard spray paint takes the place of artwork and furthers the French cafe look. The blue frame adds a dash of color to the white walls.

Menu

Jumbo Shrimp
14.99

Crawfish Étouffée
12.99

Ratatouille
11.99

Glowing report

Sconces give the bay a gentle boost of light. When the ceiling lights are turned off at night, the accent lighting sets the mood for a quiet dinner. White covers hide the electrical cords.

The color du jour is white, and the wallpaper stays. Doug makes a country kitchen disappear and pulls cafe cool out of his bag of tricks.

Easy living

Inexpensive easy-care fabrics, including mattress ticking and kitchen towels masquerading as pillow covers, communicate good looks and a relaxed attitude about spills.

DESIGNED BY **DOUG**

blue and white beauty

117

▲ If you're on a tight budget, throw in the towel—the dish towel, that is. Doug turns inexpensive kitchen towels into pillow covers on the banquette. The blue and white check pillows are perfect companions to the no-fuss mattress ticking used for the seat cushions. Dish towels are also worthy candidates for valances and cafe curtains. Use clip-on curtain rings to suspend them from a rod.

Tricked out in country blue and mauve, this kitchen seems sentenced to life in the 1980s. The owners are ready to be freed from the dated decor. Their only request is straightforward: They want Doug to strip the old wallpaper. "That will separate the men designers from the boy designers— if you take the wallpaper down instead of painting over it," says one of the owners.

Doug isn't known for abiding by the law, or at least the laws set by *Trading Spaces* homeowners. "If you think I'm going to spend two

days stripping wallpaper, you're out of your mind," he says. The wallpaper stays, but Doug doesn't paint over it. Instead he updates the walls by covering them with white paneling that mimics the look of tile. White paint freshens the oak cabinetry. Doug then takes boldness to new heights by painting the ceiling bright blue.

Although the blue ceiling ups the "wow" power of the room, the real star is the seating area located in a bay at one end of the galley-style kitchen. Doug revamps the underutilized and

Before
▶ New Orleans: Melrose Drive

Problems
▸ Bland bay area
▸ Dated wallpaper
▸ Harsh, unattractive fluorescent ceiling lights
▸ Too many items on countertops and out-of-scale objects on walls

Solutions
▸ Add a banquette that follows the angles of the bay
▸ Cover existing wallpaper with white paneling
▸ Update overhead light fixtures and hang new sconces
▸ Edit and streamline accessories

◀ With a bit of forethought, you can eke out storage space almost anywhere. Amy Wynn cut openings in the banquette bench and attached hinged cabinet doors, adding storage without giving up an inch of floor space.

Special-Effects Ceilings

For most homeowners, ceilings are an afterthought—if a thought at all. Designers, however, know that this "fifth wall" can greatly change the look, feel, and visual proportions of a room. Move beyond standard white and you'll see why this often-overlooked surface is worth your attention. Consider these tips:

▶ **High ceilings** can be visually lowered with paint that is darker than the wall color. For extra drama, use a rich, contrasting color on the ceiling (for example, partner cream-color walls with a deep purple ceiling).

▶ **Low ceilings** will seem higher if they are painted a lighter color than the walls.

▶ **Walls** make an impact on the ceiling. Vertical stripes on a wall, for example, lead the eye up to give a room the illusion of height. Adding a waist-high chair rail around a room and painting the lower walls a darker color than the upper walls will make a ceiling seem lower.

▶ **Murals, stencils, and other decorative paint techniques** are effective on ceilings as well as walls. Adding crown molding or a wallpaper border at ceiling height will also draw interest upward.

▶ **Paint the ceiling** before the walls, starting with a narrow strip at the ceiling line. Choose a roller cover with a nap appropriate for the texture of the ceiling. Use an extension pole so the majority of the painting can be done from the floor.

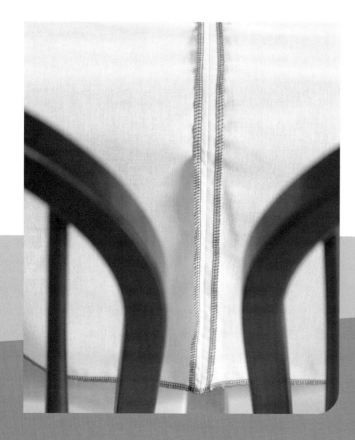

less-than-dramatic space with a banquette featuring a cushioned bench that fits snugly against the angled walls. The banquette provides more seating than individual chairs and offers a bevy of bonus storage spaces underneath. For a fun flourish, a chalkboard on one wall announces the daily specials. "I based this whole idea on a restaurant in New York," Doug explains. "We're going for this 'inside a kitchen, but inside a restaurant' sort of atmosphere."

On seeing their new room, the owners seem to have forgotten about their wallpaper request, focusing instead on another wish. "We got the window seat—yes! Yes! Yes!" one owner exclaims.

◀Blue stitching on this tablecloth makes a design statement and adds casual character befitting the overall style of the kitchen. Create a similar look by stitching together white dish towels or plain canvas, then using a contrasting thread color on the raw edges. Or, if you're after a vintage look, examine the backside of a fabric item. It may offer the ideal faded, muted colorations. Similarly, turn a shiny fabric to the flip side to tone down its glitz.

▶ elements of style

On the right track

Those familiar fluorescent light fixtures hugging the ceiling above many kitchen islands may cast the room—or its occupants—in a bad light. Easy-to-install track lights bring sleek style overhead. The individual lamps can be adjusted to shine light where it's most needed.

Fresh start

Dated cabinetry can drag a kitchen down, but paint can quickly enliven the look. Bright white paint updates this cabinetry and helps the high-rising upper cabinets blend into the ceiling, visually elevating the space.

Square pegs

Metal-covered wooden squares slip over round barstool seats to give an ordinary item unexpected new shape. The white skirts attach with hook-and-loop tape, making them easy to remove for cleaning.

positive energy

Hildi chalks up a high style score in this kitchen, designing a streamlined space with a striking black and white palette.

You are my Sunshine!

Chalk talk

Chalkboard paint is magic in a can. Roll it on walls to create a doodle-ready surface. With the wooden "valance" connecting the cabinets removed, the once-hidden wall space above this window offers an irresistible spot for spreading cheer with chalk. Removing the wooden valance also creates a more airy and streamlined look.

Tile style

Good things come to those who experiment. The backsplash and countertop look as if they have been decked out in tile. However, the material is actually a ¼-inch-thick bricklike surface typically used on floors and decks.

Shine on

This metal strip finishes the edges of the countertops in contemporary style. Exposed screws lend an industrial feel.

◄ Hildi salvaged the butcher-block top from a 2×2-foot kitchen island—a gift from the husband to the wife—and turned it into a removable cutting board. Amy Wynn cut out a section of the countertop and retrofitted it so the butcher-block top slides in and out for easy cleaning or for use elsewhere. To prepare the cabinets to accept primer, Hildi rubbed on liquid sander—an alternative to messy sandpaper. Black appliance paint makes the refrigerator less obtrusive.

Before
▶Tallahassee: Copperfield Circle

Problems
▶ **Crowded, somewhat cluttered space**
▶ **Dark walls and dark cabinetry**
▶ **Dated appliances**
▶ **Lack of visual interest; lack of energy in the space**

Solutions
▶ **Remove island; streamline everything**
▶ **Brighten the room with a color scheme of black and white**
▶ **Paint appliances**
▶ **Add playful touches, such as chalk drawings and snack-barstool skirts**

With cabinets and appliances taking up most of the wall space, you'd think a kitchen would be a breeze to decorate. Think again. "Kitchens are always more of a challenge than people think," Hildi says.

The challenge in this kitchen is to cook up a more modern look. "It's red and boring and the only room in our house that has never changed in the 10 years that we've lived here," one owner says.

Hildi can't abide boring. "I want to have a big effect on everything we touch in here," she says. Nixing the sunshine yellows and apple greens that bring cheer to many kitchens, Hildi goes in an opposite design direction, introducing a black and white scheme.

Though black is usually used in small doses to lend definition to a room, Hildi bravely smothers the kitchen walls and the adjoining dining room walls in black. It's not ordinary black; it's chalkboard paint that transforms walls into scribble-friendly surfaces—a fun idea for any kitchen that hosts children.

Armed with chalk in kid colors, Hildi and her team unleash the playful side of the room by doodling and drawing on nearly every sliver of wall space. A recipe from Hildi's father runs all the way down one narrow wall. On another wall, there's space for jotting down items needed from the store. A sun peeks out from behind the curtains. Elsewhere, sketches of fruits and farm animals provide visual interest.

The random chalk renderings and a big dollop of white keep the black from becoming oppressive. Newly painted bright-white cabinets pop out from the black background, brightening the space and energizing the black.

The high-contrast color scheme is only the beginning of Hildi's redo recipe. Streamlining is the next key ingredient. Ironically, the first thing to be whittled down is a small butcher-block island that took up too much floor space. The top is repurposed into a portable

◄ In the dining room, Hildi took out a traditional light fixture and heavy draperies to launch the update. White fabric panels are threaded on a thin metal strip to create crisp pleats; a mod pendent light adds a contemporary touch. The curtains are hung at ceiling height to make the room seem taller and more spacious.

► Metallic touches bring sparkle and contemporary flair into the kitchen. This metal strip wraps the edges of the countertops. It's a decorative touch that has a practical purpose: The strip creates a lip to corral the polymer-base cement bricks on the countertop. The ¼-inch-thick bricks, which came on pieces of meshlike tile, were adhered to the existing countertop with mastic and then grouted.

cutting board; the work area now has more elbowroom. "The family can gather in the kitchen now," Hildi says. "Before it was like ring-around-the-butcher-block."

The fluorescent ceiling light is another casualty on Hildi's hit list, as is the nondescript chandelier hanging above the dining room table. Sleek chrome fixtures step in as fitting replacements in the newly modernized spaces. Chrome reappears in the flat rod that spans the dining room windows, where crisp white panels take the place of heavy swooping draperies. New hardware chimes in on the cabinets, completing the dining room transformation.

In the kitchen, silvery metal strips wrap around the countertop, finishing the edges and neatly containing a new countertop surface, which features black and slate colorations that blend with the walls. Appliances receive a similar streamline-by-color treatment. Sprayed with black appliance paint, the formerly almond refrigerator blends into the dark background. The new black look for the cooktop also comes courtesy of paint: automotive engine enamel, which can withstand high temperatures.

"This is [a] positive-negative [color palette], but it's so positive," Hildi says of the black and white scheme.

ROOM # 35 THRIVING SPACE family

◄ A chalkboard souvenir preserves the family's experience.

► Hildi put her father's recipe in a prime spot, creating a fun backdrop for a grouping of pictures. The bright red in these photos gives them prominence against the busy background. Framing photos in wide mats can also provide visual relief.

Cabinetry Refresher Course

Kitchen cabinetry can be decorative as well as functional. If buying new cabinets is out of the question, adapt some of these strategies for your existing cabinets:

► **Furniture flair.** Decorative treatments can make cabinets look more like furniture. Moldings on upper cabinets create the look of a hutch, while legs and toe-kicks on lower cabinets create the look of freestanding furniture. Wide and deep drawers help a cabinet resemble a dresser.

► **Breaking out.** Long banks of cabinets that give way to smaller blocks create an unfitted look—a style that recalls kitchens of yesteryear. Cabinets hung alone also lend an unfitted furniture look to a kitchen.

► **Two-color treatment.** There's room for more than one color in a single cabinetry scheme. Paint the upper cabinets and leave the lower ones in their original wood stain or vice versa. Or paint upper and lower cabinets in different shades of one color or in completely different colors.

► **Maple magic.** In recent years maple has begun to rival oak as the cabinetry material of choice. Much of the popularity is due to its versatility—its natural color and grain works well with a variety of room styles and countertop materials. Rather than purchasing all new maple cabinets, however, consider painting the existing cabinet bodies and purchasing new maple doors only.

► **Changing faces.** A mix of cabinet fronts—solid doors, glass panels, or no doors at all—breaks up design monotony and offers an opportunity for introducing textured or tinted glass.

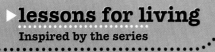
First Steps to Classic

Even if your sofa is out of style, it can become a timeless beauty if you cover and surround it with classic choices, including pinstripe fabric, rich colors (such as black, white, and taupe), and accessories with elegant shapes.

PERFECT PALETTE Taupe and white, nicely punctuated with sophisticated touches of black, are as elegant as a black-tie affair. This color combination cinches classic, lasting style.

STRIPE STRATEGY
When you're unsure about what pattern to use in your classic room, call on stripes. A combination of thick and thin stripes prevents this print from feeling static.

BEAUTY ABROAD
Imported rugs have graced venerable homes for centuries. They're prized for their gorgeous designs, rich colors, and plush feel underfoot.

Before

See the following pages for four additional options:

One Sofa, Five Ways
Inspired by the Series

HIGH-RISE Done right, black and white photography works well with any design style. This image of a gracefully curving staircase offers an updated version of architectural artwork—always considered a classic.

DRAMATIC FLAIR A softly flared shade and a turned-spindle base give this table lamp timeless appeal.

TRUE TRADITIONS Librarylike accessories, such as stacks of books and a graceful reproduction brass hourglass, make the room seem more cozy and classic.

RICH FINISH Dark wood furnishings, such as the coffee table and side tables, make a rich, bold statement. A curlicue base on one table is reminiscent of architecture salvaged from historic buildings.

Do

DESIGNED BY **CHRISTI**

Dos and Don'ts

Compatible Color

Keep colors from fighting in your home by reading up on their basic traits and qualities. Then choose your "guest list" and invite selected hues into the house.

132

◄ In Austin: Round Rock Trail, Christi borrows colors from one homeowner's beloved ceramic rooster and cheers up this kitchen with a dramatic complementary palette of red and green.

Don't

Before you buy paint, have a game plan for color selection. In the illustration *above,* for example, an open doorway necessitates compatible colors in the adjacent rooms. The pink and orange cannot happily coexist side by side, at least not in a traditional setting. Next time you hit the paint aisle, take along a color wheel (available at art stores and home centers) and keep these color guidelines in mind:

▶ **Complementary colors.** Colors that lie opposite each other on the color wheel are complementary, such as the red and green hues that Christi used in the kitchen *opposite*. When paired, each makes the other appear more vivid. (Red is an excellent choice for a kitchen—experts say it stimulates conversation and appetite!)

▶ **Analogous colors.** Hues that lie beside each other on the color wheel are analogous; they always look good together because they share a common hue.

▶ **Triads.** Any three equally spaced colors on the wheel make a lively yet balanced combination. The scheme may feel jarring unless you let one color dominate and use the other two as accents.

▶ **Temperature.** The wheel also helps you identify warm and cool hues. Half the wheel, from red to yellow-green, is considered warming, stimulating, and advancing. This description reflects emotional associations (the sun looks yellow; fire is orange and red). However, it has a basis in physiology: The eye can't bring the red and purple ends of the spectrum into focus at the same time, so it perceives red to be nearer or advancing. The other half of the wheel is home to colors described as cool; these colors appear to recede. A warm color scheme needs a dollop of a cool hue to feel well-rounded and complete; a cool color scheme needs a jolt of warm color for energy. Green and purple may seem to advance in one setting and recede in another; for that reason, some interior designers consider them neutrals that can go with any color.

DESIGNED BY **BARRY**

▼ In Tallahassee: Emerson Lane, Barry introduces a
dining spot between the kitchen and family room.
Extending a concrete tabletop perpendicular to the
cooking peninsula makes it easy to pass plates for
quick serving and cleaning up.

Floor Plan
Finesse

Create Your
Ideal Kitchen

Whip up a kitchen layout that encourages great
cooking, good conversation, and smooth traffic flow.

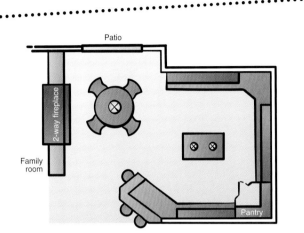

Added Ingredients

A spacious work core makes this kitchen roomy enough for a center island—a handy feature for additional storage and counter space or for gathering around during parties. Perimeter cabinetry culminates in a peninsula, which angles at 45 degrees. This angle allows plenty of floor space in the work core and brings anyone perched on the stools closer in to chat with the cook. The round table accommodates additional diners, who can enjoy a view of the two-way fireplace or the view out the patio door.

Dine In

If you prefer not to have people passing through the work core, this is a good plan for you. Locating a dining table at the center of the L-shape work core routes traffic from the adjoining space and out the patio door without anyone stepping in the way of kitchen activity. The refrigerator is located close to the traffic path so guests or children can grab a beverage without entering the work core. Three chairs are situated around the table for visitors or helpers, and the fourth chair tucks into a nearby corner to keep the work core aisle open.

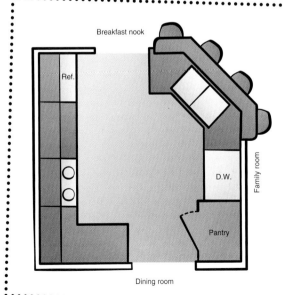

Conversation's Cooking

This kitchen could have ended up like any plain old galley, serving as a passage from the breakfast nook to the dining room. Instead the space is designed slightly wider to more comfortably accommodate multiple cooks and anyone passing through. Opening a portion of the wall between the kitchen and family room keeps the kitchen from feeling closed off from the rest of the house. Stools pulled up to the angled counter are convenient for quick snacks and conversation with the cook. The dining areas flanking the work core are easily accessible for serving and cleaning up.

DESIGNED BY DOUG

◀ In Austin: Round Rock Trail, Doug adds style and storage to a bedroom with these angular shelves custom-built by Carter. Painting the interior back of the shelves bold blue introduces a striking accent color that sets off any items on display. When you plan to paint wood pieces such as these, use less-expensive materials, such as pine or MDF.

To gauge the quality of wood furniture, you need to know a little about wood types and construction techniques. Knowing about the different types of wood materials will also help you make good choices if you want to build your own furniture.

Wood Types

Hardwoods are more durable than softwoods and are typically more expensive. Colors range widely among woods—even those of the same species—and various woods can be stained or bleached to alter the original color.

Among all the hardwoods, cherry, maple, mahogany, oak, teak, and walnut are prized for fine furniture. See the plank photo *opposite* for a rundown on common hardwoods. (Note: White pine, a softwood, is also shown in the photo.)

Softwoods

More available than hardwoods, softwoods are typically less expensive and can be a good choice for wood furniture that you buy or build, depending on use and preference. Softwoods require extra care to avoid marring or denting the surface.

▶ **Pine (white).** Because it was readily available and easy to work with, white pine was used for many primitive pieces. Many of these old

Smart Buys

Wood Furniture

Whether you are purchasing a new or vintage item, choosing good looks is a given. Selecting a long-lasting, quality furniture piece takes a bit more thought.

pieces show traces of wear because of the softness of the wood. Vintage pieces are valued for their patina and reasonable cost.

▸ **Pine (yellow).** This wood is grainy and does not finish well. It is a poor choice for exposed wood.

Composites

Composites are manufactured wood products typically used for shelving, back panels of furniture pieces, and some modern styles of furniture. Prices and performance vary.

▸ **Plywood** ranges from white to tan and features multiple layers of thin wood sheets that are glued and pressed together. It is strong and resistant to warping, shrinking, and swelling. In furniture, plywood is most often used as supporting members. Some contemporary furniture is manufactured from plywood, which can be shaped and bent into permanent contours.

▸ **Particleboard** is usually light brown to medium brown. It is made of sawdust, small wood chips, and glue or resin that have been mixed together and pressure-treated. It is a common component of inexpensive furniture, usually covered with laminate or veneer.

A MAPLE Light beige to tan. Good resistance to shrinking, warping, and wear. Very hard. Difficult to detail; sometimes dyed.

B CHERRY Reddish brown. Good resistance to shrinking, swelling, and warping; dyes well. Easy to detail for decorative carving.

C PINE Clear, near white. Poor resistance to shrinking, swelling, and warping. Soft grain; easy to work with but not always durable.

D MAHOGANY Reddish brown to red. Good resistance to shrinking and warping. Softer hardwood, easy to detail for carving. Takes rich, dark stains.

E WALNUT Dark grayish brown. Often stained darker. Good resistance to swelling and warping. Takes stains evenly and is easy to carve.

F OAK Light pinkish brown. Good resistance to shrinking and warping. Takes stains evenly and is very easy to carve for detailing.

It splits easily, and the veneer or laminate may pop loose when the particleboard swells and shrinks with moisture changes. A similar product called hardboard is made under higher pressure, which creates an improved product.

▸ **MDF, or medium-density fiberboard,** is made of wood particles that are bonded with resin and compressed. The material is hard and can be cut and used like plywood. However, it isn't as strong as plywood. Still, you'll pay less for MDF, which costs about $15 for a ½-inch-thick 4×8-foot sheet. You can paint plain MDF, or purchase MDF covered with melamine—a durable plastic surface that comes in a variety of colors. Because exposed edges of MDF are rough, plan to finish them with molding or 1× lumber.

Construction Techniques

tip

The methods used to assemble furniture determine its durability. Joints should be mortise-and-tenon or joined with dowels and should be stable and secure. Butted and mitered joints are weaker and won't stand up to heavy wear unless reinforced. Table legs and chair legs should be reinforced with triangular or diagonal blocks of wood that keep joints square and help stabilize the furniture when it is moved or when pressure is applied to the surface. To check for stability, apply pressure at the diagonals.

A

DESIGNED BY CHRISTI

Style Primer

Classic

Think of designs that withstand the test of time and you'll get the picture regarding classic style. In New Orleans: Carriage Road, Christi resurrects a French Quarter classic.

Historical Hues

Muted tones, such as the soft yellow on these dining room walls, look earthy and worn—as if they've been around for decades. For a vintage look, generally stay away from clear, bright primary colors. Check the paint aisle at your home center for manufacturers of historical paint hues; most produce brochures and color cards to help you choose classic colors that will work anywhere in the house. Ⓐ

Aged in an Instant

Give colors a nudge into the past with special aging techniques. After the new paint on this furniture dried, for example, Christi and her team lightly sanded the edges to create a worn, aged look. To make freshly painted furniture appear older, brush dark stain over the paint and then partially rub it off with rags, allowing the stain to streak the finish and settle into recessed areas. Ⓓ Ⓕ

Ancient Walls

Have you ever seen an old building where plaster is peeling off the walls, revealing the bricks below? For this dining room, Christi says she wants to create the look of "an old European village," beginning with random patches of thin faux bricks, which are applied to the walls with tile mastic. Joint compound is tinted with yellow paint, and play sand is added to give it texture. When the joint compound is trowelled to the walls abutting the brick patches, the walls take on the appearance of old peeling plaster over brick. Ⓑ

139

Salvaged Style An antique serving sideboard would break the budget, so Christi devises an antique look for a piece custom-built by Amy Wynn. Two beefy turned legs were once the posts on an old bed. The serving piece is painted and stained to blend with the rest of the dining room furniture. Ⓒ Ⓗ

Repurposed Pleasures Christi keeps the existing table, chairs, and chandelier, painting and staining the pieces to fit the classic look. To make the shiny brass chandelier as attractive as the rest of the furnishings, Christi sponges on different colors of paint mixed with sand for a textural finish. Finishing the dry paint with dark stain makes the fixture look old. Crystal drops on the arms add a note of old-world elegance. Ⓔ

Cultural Connection Artwork in a classically styled room can complement the period or region you have in mind. Christi plays up the French Quarter classic theme of this New Orleans-area home with artwork fashioned from a decorative mask, an intricate wood onlay, and a reproduction tin ceiling tile. Ⓑ

Fabric Finery Lightweight fabrics with a sheen distinguish the windows. Lengths of gold, rose, and silver duppioni silk form the luxurious draperies. Christi uses more fabric to cover the drop chain on the chandelier. Fabric stores offer all kinds of cloth that can suit a classic look, including toile, ticking, and damask. Ⓐ Ⓖ

Anytime you can carve more than one function out of a single room, give yourself a pat on the back. After all, the minimum cost for adding on a bare-bones room to your existing home is significant. So if you're hoping for a home office or saving up for a sitting room, put away your checkbook and open up your mind: The space you need could be in the bedroom. Follow the lead of the *Trading Spaces* designers and transform a slice of space into a nice place to read, watch TV, or work. Oh, and don't forget to pat yourself on the back for saving all that money!

dual-pur
bed

pose
rooms

Royal flush
Purple makes its regal debut on the walls in the sitting area to further differentiate the two spaces. The saturated hue contrasts with the green walls in the sleeping area.

Wraparound
Cording stands in for crown molding to add architectural interest where there was none. The cording was simply hot-glued in one long strip around the perimeter of the room.

Mantel makeover
A sleek new mantel and pillars that bump out from an awkward angled wall bring stature to the fireplace, the focal point of the sitting area. A new entertainment center flows from the reconfigured fireplace and mimics its clean lines.

Blissful slumber
Shimmering fabrics and plump pillows give the bed a starring role.

DESIGNED BY **EDWARD**

split decision

Divided attention

Floor-to-ceiling panels separate the large room into two smaller spaces, one for sleeping and one for reading, relaxing, or watching television. Sheer fabric panels prevent the partitions from seeming obtrusive.

Canopy class

This metal canopy is actually a pot rack. With yards of flowing fabric cascading from it, the utilitarian kitchen item seems tailor-made for its new role above the bed.

This big master suite was an introvert when its owners wanted an extrovert. Edward perks up the room by creating separate spaces for sleeping and relaxing and introducing color, texture, and a bit of the unexpected.

▼ Less can be more. This single white orchid in a clear glass vase is striking in its simplicity.

Before
Nashville: Cold Stream Drive

Problems
- Large, underutilized room
- No color
- Nondescript fireplace with a small mantel and no surround
- Limited options for positioning furniture; only one option for placing the bed

Solutions
- Add function by dividing the room into two areas: one for sleeping and one for relaxing
- Bring in color with paint and fabrics
- Build a larger mantel and add columns to the fireplace to give it character
- Because the bed must remain in its highly visible position, make it a worthy focal point

◄ This display pedestal bridges the gap between the new mantel and the entertainment center, easing the transition between the two walls. Painted black, the entire fireplace unit visually recedes into the purple wall. If your room has an architectural detail you want to emphasize, paint it a color that contrasts with the wall. For example, painting the entertainment center white would have increased its presence in the room.

ntil Edward came along, the owners of this master bedroom were starting to think that bigger wasn't necessarily better. Though their room is grand in size, it is bland in style. Its plain vanilla walls are misfits in a house brimming with color, and its timid personality doesn't reflect the couple's image. "The room is boring," says one owner. "And we're not boring," the other quickly chimes in.

The need for color is obvious. Edward's design will involve much more than that, however. He decides to use rich purple and earthy hues. "We've got basically two rooms to do here," Edward says.

Room One is the sleeping area. Because only one wall can accommodate the bed, Edward's options are limited. "I couldn't really move the furniture around in this room, and that's normally where you get the biggest dramatic change," he says. Resourceful as ever, Edward brings the drama to the bed by cocooning it with a canopy of flowing fabric. The pinnacle for Edward's cost-conscious canopy is actually an iron pot rack in disguise.

Room Two is the sitting area, a space Edward defines with two floor-to-ceiling panels. The trouble spot in this area is an angled wall that houses a lackluster fireplace with a wimpy mantel. With Amy Wynn's help, the fireplace now boasts clean-lined columns and a bolder mantel that flows into an entertainment center on the adjacent wall.

Though he divides the space by function, Edward treats the room as a whole. Greens and purples weave throughout each area, appearing

▶ Hanging curtain panels at the ceiling line rather than right above the window is a foolproof design trick that adds the illusion of height. Ready-mades may need some extra length to reach the floor. Edward lengthened standard 84-inch panels for the windows in this sitting area. He purchased an extra set of draperies, cut off a portion of each panel, and sewed the pieces onto the first set. Tasseled trim camouflages the seams.

147

◄ With a relatively low headboard, this bed lacked impact. Edward's ingenious solution is a canopy created from a $40 pot rack. The retrofitted rack hangs from the ceiling and supports yards of flowing fabric gracefully pulled back to frame the bed. The fabric attaches to curtain ring clips on a rod hung on the wall behind the bed. The same sheer fabric used for the partitions creates a soft backdrop above the headboard. Lamps mounted directly to the wall provide light for nighttime reading and ensure that there's one less thing cluttering the nightstands.

in varying amounts for interest. Fabrics, including fashionable new window treatments, also unite the two areas. Orchids and spiky greenery give the room a subtle outdoorsy feel that veers toward exotic.

Turning one room into two didn't mean Edward could double his $1,000 budget. When it was all tallied, though, he had nearly $30 to spare—an amazing design feat considering what the owners got: a sitting room outfitted with a more attractive fireplace and an entertainment center, as well as a dramatic and inviting sleeping area.

Sleep in Style

Regardless of size—twin, queen, king, or other—a bed is typically the focal point in any bedroom. You spend about one-third of your life in bed, so why not spend it in style? Think back to a stay at a favorite hotel or bed-and-breakfast, and then apply some of those pampering amenities to your own setting. These ideas will get you started:

▶ **Comfort and cocoon with canopies.** If you don't have a four-poster to drape fabric over, create a similar effect by hanging curtains or fabric from ceiling-mounted drapery rods or towel rings. A wall-mounted corona, typically a half-circle crown affixed high on the wall and draped with fabric, is another option. Large quilting hoops or finials designed for window scarves will also serve the purpose.

▶ **Add a second box spring** to give a tired bed greater presence. Layering a feather bed on top of a mattress also fluffs up a bed, adding luxury that is both physically comforting and visually appealing. Additional layers of decorative shams and pillows have a similar effect.

▶ **Soften the expanse of wall behind a bed** by shirring fabric on a curtain rod or by hanging a quilt or tapestry rug on the wall.

▶ **Give your room a new outlook** by changing the bedding with the seasons. A reversible comforter is a budget-friendly way to keep your surroundings interesting. In the summer, some sheets are pretty enough to be used alone; put the comforter or duvet at the foot of the bed until cooler weather returns.

▲ Spray-painted gold and plumped with a purple cushion, an outdoor chaise beckons from its new indoor locale. Edward spotted the chaise on the deck of his team members, who donated it to the cause.

Look here
Bold red squares of color on the walls and matching shelves immediately draw attention to the playful displays of sports collectibles. The squares add clean-lined, graphic appeal to the room.

Simple setting
Taupe provides a warm, uncomplicated backdrop for the various collections. The gentle hue balances the strong red accents.

Romantic glow
Though this bedroom can function as an office by day (a desk is tucked into one corner), it turns romantic by night with the help of these candles.

DESIGNED BY **VERN**

Color continuity
The red and taupe palette continues to the bed, where silky fabrics add luxury.

cache conscious

Lights, please

A pair of lamps prevents the showcased collection from lurking in the shadows. The lamp base and shade have clean lines that recede into the quiet backdrop.

Can a bedroom be livable and yet lavished in tchotchkes? Follow Vern's lead as he sorts out the cache of collectibles in this boudoir and makes the space more beautiful with storage, bold red accents, and a wood floor. He even makes room for an office!

No dust

A custom-made bookcase looks elegant in black and offers the ideal backdrop for showing off the owner's collection of snow globes. Clear acrylic-panel doors keep the dust out.

ern is known for his clean, uncluttered designs, so this bedroom is a special challenge, filled to the brim with collections of all kinds, including bobble-head dolls and an enormous quantity of snow globes. "We love our junk," confesses one of the owners. "Basically our entire house is devoted to kids. We'd like to have a room devoted to us."

Vern rises to the occasion by editing the collections and displaying them in custom-made cases and on wall-mounted shelves. "Some of this has got to get out of this room," he says. "I know it is important to them, so we'll bring some back in."

To prepare for the reentry of selected collectibles, Vern establishes a quiet background with taupe paint. Building wall shelves without backs saves time and money; red squares painted on the walls serve as graphic matching backgrounds for the red-painted shelves. Vern says he designed the shelves "as a cool way to display their stuff." He then decrees, "This is where Tchotchke Land is going to happen." Sports collectibles are stowed in three of the shadow boxes, and snow globes take center stage in the remaining three.

Next, the ancient carpeting goes. In its place, an elegant wood parquet tile floor—purchased for a mere $1 per square foot— provides visual warmth. "It's one of the affordable ways to install

▶ Because this shadow box lacks a back, it's easy to build using 1× lumber and finishing nails. To create a similar display space, paint the wall behind the shelf to match or contrast. For a textural backdrop, apply fabric, art paper, or burlap to the wall.

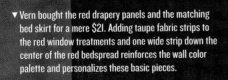
▼ Vern bought the red drapery panels and the matching bed skirt for a mere $21. Adding taupe fabric strips to the red window treatments and one wide strip down the center of the red bedspread reinforces the wall color palette and personalizes these basic pieces.

◄ The bookcase, custom-built by Amy Wynn, keeps cherished items on display; clear acrylic panels protect the collectibles from dust. If you lack the skills to build a cabinet like this one, mount legs on purchased cubes and place the cubes side by side.

top. The bedroom can now serve as a quiet place to pay bills or work at home during the day.

A bookcase, built long and low like the dressers, stands beneath the remaining three red shelves. Snow globes fill the new storage; clear acrylic-panel doors minimize dusting.

Vern centers the bed on a window, which makes the room feel more spacious and creates a focal point. Luxurious red and taupe drapery panels stand in as a headboard. Vern embellishes the silky red bedspread with a matching stripe of taupe fabric down the center to visually link the linens to the window.

Vern sums up his assignment: "I think I was put into the room deliberately to test me," he says, smiling.

The owners are all smiles too. They thought that Vern might jettison their belongings in a garage sale. Relieved and ecstatic, they offer him kudos: "This is so, so awesome," says one owner. "It is gorgeous. Thank you, Vern!"

wood flooring in a room when you're on a tight budget," Vern says. "But installing it takes a bit of effort."

Vern then devises a better furniture arrangement. Below one set of shelves, in an alcove once occupied by the bed, he positions two existing black dressers, substituting handsome silver knobs for the old plastic ones. He bridges the gap between the dressers with a black-painted shelf to create a streamlined computer desk

Tips for Tidying Up

Unless you constantly strive to be neat and tidy in the bedroom, it's easy to let down your guard and give in to clutter and chaos. If you get a handle on organization, however, you'll be on the way to creating a peaceful, livable retreat. Here are some ideas for space-saving storage:

▶ **Choose clothes hampers** that are too handsome to hide. They keep dirty clothes out of sight and organized for the laundry. Buy two: one for washable clothing and one for dry cleaning.

▶ **In a bedroom with little or no storage,** use decorative storage cubes with removable lids. Position them at bedside as nightstands or at the foot of the bed in place of a more conventional blanket chest.

▶ **Use the space under a bed** for heavy-duty plastic or cardboard storage boxes. This strategy works well for out-of-season items, such as sweaters or blankets. Use underbed storage for archived belongings that require climate control, such as photographs, books, and heirloom linens.

▶ **Skirt a particleboard table** and use the space underneath for stacked boxes. Some plywood table bases are made with a shelf for stowing stacked storage boxes. Alternatively, add a wood bench and use the space underneath the seat to stash out-of-season items in wicker suitcases or in decorative boxes.

▶ **If space allows, use the most classic storage of all:** the desk. Vern added desktop space to this bedroom by placing a shelf across two existing dressers. A small writing table can also work if your storage needs are minimal.

▶ **Use a bedroom wall** for floor-to-ceiling bookshelves. Shelves can even be built over the tops of windows and doors for additional storage. Adjustable shelves and a few drawers or cupboards make a shelving unit more versatile.

▲ To create a desk in only a few hours, leave a space between two dressers or filing cabinets. Top the cabinets or dressers with a prefabricated wood shelf that's stained or painted to match (or cut a shelf from MDF and paint it). The space between the two desktop supports serves as the kneehole.

Lighten up
Massive black furnishings can seem forbidding. The pale wood tone of this cabinet door lightens the look.

Dressed up
To get maximum mileage out of existing furnishings, factor them into a new design. Painted black, this dresser blends with the desk unit and functions as an integral part of the piece.

Study hall
Like a study cube in a college library, this desk seems shut off from the world. A quiet place for reading, writing, or paying bills can be carved out of even the tiniest space.

DESIGNED BY FRANK

comfort-plus bedroom

Going solo

Not every wall has to be the same color. Painting one wall this brown hue gives it instant authority, designating it as a focal point.

Doubling up

Two pictures, two bedside lamps, two shelving units. Symmetry adds to the serene and orderly feel. The prints are enlarged copyright-free architectural drawings. To age this affordable artwork, crumple the paper and/or lightly brush it with a tea-stain or paint diluted with water.

Custom touch

Inexpensive shelves—even the kind designed for use in a basement or garage—can be made to look better with a few custom touches. A two-tone treatment makes this commercial shelving unit more stylish.

Suspended in space

If you lack space for a traditional bedside table, a small shelf mounted on the wall or on another nearby vertical surface will serve equally well.

This bedroom has a just-moved-in feel to it. It lacks color, pattern, artwork, and atmosphere. Frank gives it a homey, lived-in look using rich color, interesting fabrics, and a superfunctional librarylike shelving unit.

▲ To reduce Carter's carpentry load, Frank purchased this no-frills shelf (and the matching one on the other side of the bed) and had Carter modify it to work in this space. A two-tone treatment dresses it up, and a side ledge acts as a nightstand. The metal X in the back is an industrial support that bolsters both the frame and the contemporary flair of the remade room.

▶ Whether it's used to serve breakfast in bed or to hold letters, this tray is a special reminder of good friends and good times. To make a similar tray for a friend, purchase an inexpensive unfinished wood tray, paint it, and use a marker or paint pen to write a message. To protect the surface, apply clear polyurethane.

The old adage that you need to be comfortable in your own skin applies to decorating too: A room may look good and function well, yet unless it feels comfortable to you, you'll be uneasy in the space. These owners know their comfort level: They want their bedroom to feel warm and be a relaxing place to hang out, much like the coffeehouses they frequent. "But we don't want a coffee shop in our room," one owner adds.

Frank comes up with a vigorous plan to give the owners a multifunctional room that accommodates their love of reading and writing and exudes the ambience of a coffeehouse. Part One of his three-pronged approach is the sleeping area. A bedding ensemble in russet and other brown hues launches the warm color scheme. The wall behind the bed is painted reddish brown for instant impact. The color creates a dramatic backdrop for the contrasting wooden bed, which is flanked by tall bookshelves. The other walls wear a coat of light taupe.

Part Two is a sitting area. Two wicker chairs designed for outdoor use create a casual place for reading. Placed in front of a window, the chairs look right at home as they bask in natural light.

Part Three is Frank's grand finale: a wall-spanning library. The library wall hosts two desks, bookshelves, and a cabinet that keeps clutter out of view. The custom-built storage unit is a welcome addition in a formerly disorganized space. It was definitely worth

▲ Blocks are fun at any age. Four blocks cut from 4×4s and embellished with letters make for an adult-friendly decoration. Wood accessories and furnishings help create the feel of a coffeehouse, where natural wood is often incorporated into the decor.

Before
▶ Austin: Mather Trail

Problems
▶ Disorganization; lack of storage
▶ A solitary icy blue wall and a generally barren look
▶ Room had limited functionality and underutilized space

Solutions
▶ Build shelves to display personalized accessories
▶ Add warmth through fabrics and paint the blue wall a rich brown color
▶ Build a library with desks and shelves to accommodate the owners' interest in reading and writing

159

Double Decisions

Even if you have a tiny berth as a bedroom, it can function as more than mere sleeping space. Consider these options:

▶ **Create a mini "stage set"** by carefully grouping furniture. Two small chairs placed in front of a window create the illusion of a separate sitting area. A cushioned bench placed at the foot of the bed has a similar effect.

▶ **Visually define distinct areas** with rugs, folding screens, or an accent wall color. If space permits, pull the bed out from a wall and position it in the center of the room; the area behind the bed becomes almost like a separate room.

▶ **Use furnishings that serve multiple purposes.** A writing table can double as a vanity, and an armoire can hold a television and out-of-season clothing.

▶ **Put the closet to good use.** Remove double doors and use the closet space as a miniature office or sitting area—or a showy spot for a dresser. If you can't spare the closet space, dress up the closet entrance with curtain panels draped to the side. This treatment gives the illusion that something grand is beyond.

▲ "It was all about reading," Frank says of the room. These letter-embellished wood pieces back up his claim. Wood blocks, cardboard storage boxes, and many other objects can be embellished with letters that spell out a special message. Look for paper or wood cutouts at crafts stores; if you're a numbers person, metal house numbers from a home center may suit your style.

▲ Cream-color fringe lends definition between the comforter and matching pillow. Bedding ensembles are an easy starting point for any bedroom's design. Gussy up plain pillows or bed skirts with trims that can be secured with fabric glue.

▶ The outdoor furniture section of a home center or discount store offers great finds for indoor use; if you shop at the right time, you can get end-of-season bargains. This white wicker chair brings texture and color contrast into the room. It's also lightweight enough to move if needed elsewhere in the room or anywhere in the house.

the effort to lug the sections up the stairs, but Frank says jokingly, "I know what those Egyptians felt like when building a pyramid."

The storage story continues with a five-drawer dresser that tucks under the library cabinet, between the desks. Another dresser sits between the wicker chairs, where an end table might typically be found. Wicker baskets on the bedside bookshelves can store socks or other garments if all the dresser drawers fill up.

"This is $995.71 worth of brand-new master bedroom," Paige says, referring to the bounty of new furnishings and accessories Frank brought into the space. That leaves almost enough money for a couple of lattes.

Taking in the warm colors and wooden accessories during the Reveal, the owners feel transported to a coffeehouse, their favorite place for relaxation and reading. "This is exactly what we said," one owner remarks. "I always wanted a pretty room, and we have a pretty room."

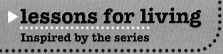
First Steps to
Chic

Do you want to take your living room from sad to chic? Use this handy makeover map to infuse your space with sleek style, from clean-lined furnishings to accessories with contemporary flair.

SHADE CHIC Stylish lamps make a cool and sophisticated design statement. This modern rendition features a shade that's artistic and unusual.

GREEN SCENE
An extra-long skirt and rich sage green fabric make the sofa slipcover appear plush and welcoming. Beaded fringe subtly accessorizes the seating like a string of pearls paired with a little black dress.

DEEP THOUGHTS A fuzzy area rug and the fluffy cover on one pillow prevent the setting from seeming too serious. Sink-in soft materials such as these ensure that your chic design isn't elitist.

Before

See the following
pages for four
additional options:
32, Casual
64, Romantic
96, Funky
130, Classic

One Sofa, Five Ways Inspired by the Series

ABSTRACT IDEA
Contemporary art fits the theme and
introduces a dramatic dose of color
without being gaudy. The clean-lined
black frame and white mat let the art
speak for itself.

WORLDLY WAYS Introduce accessories
that embrace culture, handcrafted skills, and knowledge.
Here, an Asian-style obelisk, thrown pottery, and antique
books say "chic retreat."

FINE FLAIR Straight, clean lines are
the order of the day, but toss in a little softness
to ensure that the room doesn't feel stiff. The
handsome side tables have a straightforward
look; their legs end in a subtle, graceful flare.

OTTOMAN EMPIRE Chic design is practical
and stylish in equal measure. This round ottoman looks
fabulous functioning as a coffee table. Remove the tray and
it's also useful as a footrest or an additional seat.

DESIGNED BY **KIA**

Do

Dos
and
Don'ts

A Sense of Scale

Color, pattern, and texture are only part of a complete
decorating plan. Scale rounds out the package, and it pays to
understand this relatively abstract element of design.

164

Don't

◄ In Atlanta: Bluffview Drive, Kia takes advantage of a voluminous bedroom, creating a grand focal point with this substantial custom-made canopy bed. Designs cut into the wooden canopy make the bed a piece of artwork in its own right.

f you've ever noticed a piece of furniture looking lost in a room, you already know something about scale. Scale is the relationship between the size of a room and the objects in it, and it has a significant effect on the appeal of a space.

When the *Trading Spaces* designers visit homes, one of the most common decorating problems they see is furniture, artwork, and other objects that are way too large or far too small for the space they occupy.

Look at the room in the illustration *above*. The room has only a modest amount of square footage; however, its high ceiling yields impressive volume. All the decorating don'ts—the wall art, the side table, the lamp, the coffee table, and the rug fall into that negative category because they are relatively small and look awkward and inadequate in the space.

In this case, it's easy to replace don'ts with dos: Replace the artwork with one extra-large piece or a number of medium-size pieces arranged in one large grouping. Trade the tiny side table for something more substantial. Substitute a rug that's at least as wide as the sofa (or in a bedroom, at least as long as the bed) so it can anchor the space. If the rug is too small, it will look like a lonely island amid a sea of flooring.

Kia did a great job of creating an impressive focal point in the master bedroom *opposite*. Like the room in the illustration, this bedroom boasted volume, so it needed a tall, striking bed to create a sense of drama and intimacy.

DESIGNED BY FRANK

▼ It takes only a sliver of space to make a comfortable spot for reading. In Houston: Mulberry Hill Lane, Frank creates a windowside seating area composed of two petite wicker chairs and a rolling ottoman.

Arranging Dual-Purpose Bedrooms

Floor Plan Finesse

Use these smart floor plan ideas to make your bedroom into a multifunctional space that can be used throughout the day.

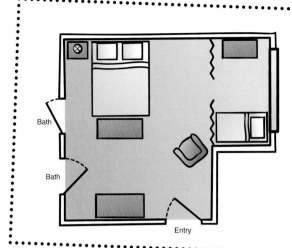

Baby Makes Three

Any new parent can tell you that dashing down the hall or upstairs to the nursery for midnight feedings is a real eye-opener. To make your nights—and Baby's—less disruptive, use this temporary arrangement until your infant is sleeping through the night. Transform a sitting area nook into a spot for the crib and changing table. Hang curtains to close off the nook at bedtime. A rocking chair outside the space accommodates late-night nursing and provides a place for bedtime stories.

Sitting on the Curve

Many larger new homes and some older homes have an architectural bonus in the bedroom: a bumped out bay with a fireplace. This floor plan logically uses the space as a sitting area but takes a softer-than-standard approach by introducing a number of gentle curves. Instead of a straight-line sofa or a pair of chairs, this arrangement employs a round rug, a round ottoman, and a kidney-shape sofa that is angled to preserve the view of the fireplace from the bed. A bench at the foot of the bed provides a place to sit and put on shoes. Opposite the bed, a pair of armoires fills out the long wall, providing more interest and more storage than a single oversize entertainment cabinet and shelves.

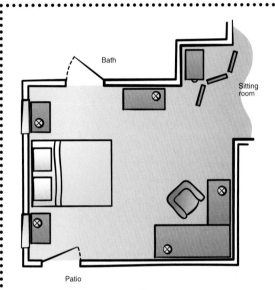

Carve a Corner Office

If you've always wanted a corner office, this floor plan can make your dream come true. Success begins in the bedroom closet (which is in the bathroom of this master suite). Free up bedroom floor space by equipping the closet to hold more, using storage add-ons such as pullout bins to take the place of dresser drawers. The storage piece shown beside the bathroom door is a tall armoire for the television. Purchase an armoire with drawers for additional in-room storage. Use the free corner for a pair of desk tops mounted on desk drawers or filing cabinets. The jog in the wall near the sitting room is ideal for tucking in another filing cabinet. A folding screen keeps the cabinet out of sight yet easily accessible.

DESIGNED BY **BARRY**

◀ In Tampa/St. Pete: Bay Laurel Court, Barry takes a girl's bedroom from toddler-style to teenage-hip, using a mix of grown-up fabrics including velvet and silk.

Smart Buys

Fabric

The material you choose for your window treatments, upholstered furnishings, and accessories affects the appearance of your room, perhaps more than any other design component. The information in this section will help you make wise selections.

The right fabrics can make a room look fabulous. If you have a tight budget, make the most of chic designer fabrics by reserving them for accents such as pillows and valances. Choose more-affordable decorator fabrics for larger items such as sofas, draperies, and slipcovers.

Though more costly than garment fabrics, decorator fabrics have higher thread counts, tighter weaves, and more weight for longer wear, so they're the best choice for items that will be used frequently. Because decorator fabrics are sold in 54-inch widths, you'll need less yardage than you would with standard 45-inch-wide garment fabrics because you get more fabric per yard. The type of fiber and the weave you select also affects how your upholstery, window treatments, and other fabric furnishings wear.

Fibers

▶ **Synthetics.** Nylon, rayon, polyester, acrylic, and olefin are all synthetic (man-made) fibers. These fibers wear well and tend to be naturally stain-resistant. Lower-quality fibers may pill.

▶ **Natural fibers.** Cotton, silk, wool, and linen are used alone or, for improved durability, blended with synthetics. They are less likely to pill than synthetics. Blends of natural fibers, particularly cotton and linen, are often used for upholstery.

Fabric Weaves

▶ **Brocade.** A weighty fabric made of cotton, wool, or silk, brocade features a raised floral design that resembles embroidery. This fabric hides dirt well and suits romantic- and classic-style rooms.

▶ **Canvas and sailcloth.** These heavy cotton fabrics are especially durable and affordable. However, the flat surface shows grime, and the heavy weave may hold dirt. Use canvas or sailcloth in rooms with casual, chic, or funky style.

▶ **Chintz.** This lighter-weight cotton may not wear as well as canvas, but the shiny finish and tight weave of the threads help resist soiling. Generally, chintz is patterned, so it hides small stains and dust. Tightly woven chintz may help spills bead up, so stains can be avoided. Enjoy this fabric in romantic- or classic-style rooms.

▶ **Damask.** Made from a weave of cotton, silk, or wool, damask is known for its textural matte-and-satin contrast. Choose tightly woven damasks without any loose threads that may snag. Damask works well in classic and romantic designs.

▶ **Lace.** Made from cotton or a cotton-polyester blend, this popular fabric features a crochetlike or eyelet design. Lace is a popular choice for window treatments, decorative pillows, and tablecloths in romantically styled rooms.

▶ **Moiré.** Made from silk or a synthetic, this fabric is coated with a finish that resembles watermarking. It is typically used for draperies, bedding, pillows, and tablecloths in chic or classic decorating schemes.

▶ **Muslin.** Also known as voile, muslin is woven from cotton with a texture that ranges from coarse to fine. It's a low-cost fabric that is often used to make slipcover patterns. It can also dress up windows or slipcover furniture in rooms with casual or funky style.

▶ **Velvet.** Woven of silk, cotton, linen, rayon, wool, or blends, velvet features a furlike feel and is heavy enough to block drafts and light. Many napped fabrics crush, making velvet a poor choice for high-use furniture. Incorporate velvet via pillows and draperies in rooms that are romantic, classic, funky, or chic.

Upholstery Fabrics

Here's the lowdown on some popular upholstery fabrics (from the top):

▶ **Wool.** Wools and wool blends are sturdy and durable enough to use for sofas and chairs. Blends can be spot-cleaned when necessary.

▶ **Vinyl.** Easier to care for and less expensive than leather, vinyls are ideal for busy living and dining areas. Unlike quality leathers, vinyls tend to stiffen and tear over time.

▶ **Cotton.** Durability depends on the weave and finish. Damask weaves are formal; canvas works for casual settings. Stain-resistant fabric protectors can help keep the fabric looking clean.

▶ **Linen.** This fiber is best suited for formal living rooms or adult areas. Have soiled pieces professionally cleaned.

▶ **Cotton blend.** Depending on the weave, this can be a sturdy, child-friendly fabric. If a blend will get everyday use, an application of stain-resistant fabric protector is a must.

▶ **Leather.** This tough material can be gently vacuumed, damp-wiped as needed, and cleaned with leather conditioners and saddle soap.

▶ **Silk.** This delicate fabric is suitable for adult areas only. It must be professionally cleaned if soiled.

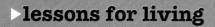

DESIGNED BY **HILDI**

Style Primer

Chic

Ⓐ

Smart, sophisticated, and current—chic interior design is all these things and more. Watch how Hildi produces this chic, sleek bedroom in Houston: Mulberry Hill Lane. Then adapt the ideas for any room in your house.

Clear Color If one thing is clear about chic style, it's color. Choose pure shades to make an unforgettable impression. Bright magenta makes a bold contemporary statement in this master bedroom; reds, oranges, blues, and greens produce equally effective results. **(A)**

Crisp White Make your main color more prominent with abundant touches of room-brightening white. Here, the bed platform, a variety of tables, and seating all stand out in white without overpowering the room. If major furnishings are white, the color options for the rest of the space are countless. **(A) (B) (E)**

Large Scale The magenta hue is an attention-getter; on an overscale headboard it demands complete attention. An extra-large armoire or artwork with generous dimensions can make a powerful impression as well. **(A)**

Geometry Lesson
Squares and rectangles repeat throughout the room to create drama. Even a striped fabric is sewn together to form a concentric square design on the toss pillows. **(C)**

Elegant Background

Soft gray suits the chic palette too. In this bedroom, the walls are wrapped in a sophisticated shade of gray to prevent the space from feeling cold. The soft neutral provides a quiet backdrop for furniture and fabrics. (A) (E)

Unfettered Lines So

where are the curlicue designs? You generally won't find them in chic style. Note the sleek, unaffected lines of the headboard, the platform bed, and the bench beneath the window. The directive here: Think straight or with gentle curves. (A) (D)

In Balance Zen is a

good word to keep in mind when developing a chic space. The look is calm and usually balanced. Repetition and precise alignment also play a role, as illustrated by the artwork and the hand-painted flower containers. (E) (F)

▶ index

Trading Spaces
Rooms for Living

Use the following index as your handy guide to locating the topics, tools, looks, styles, and designers you're looking for. Jump in!

175

The reveal.

Are you ready
to see your new room?

**With Trading Spaces books,
you'll learn techniques and gain confidence
to redecorate a room like the pros.**

Trading Spaces ™

·········· **Now Available** ··········

TLC
LIFE**UNSCRIPTED** ™